A DEEP DIVE INTO THE WORLD

MASTERING SYBASE ASE

FROM BASICS TO VERSION 16.0

By CHIDANANDA MURTHY

A DEEP DIVE INTO THE WORLD OF SYBASE

MASTERING SYBASE ASE

FROM BASICS TO VERSION 16.0

Printed in India

First Printing, 2024

ISBN **978-93-341-1865-0**

Publisher Name:
Ahana Systems & Solutions Pvt Ltd
502/37, 2nd Floor, 1st Main Rd, 8th Block, Jayanagar, Bengaluru, Karnataka 560070
India

Dedication

Dedicated to all my students, my colleagues and ex-colleagues,
my mentors and last but not the least, my family.

Without their patience, understanding, support and most above all love,
the completion of this work would not have been possible.

ACKNOWLEDGEMENTS

I would like to express my gratitude to the many people who saw me through this book; to all those who provided support, talked things over, read, wrote, offered comments, allowed me to quote their remarks and assisted in the editing, proofreading and design.

Nobody has been more important to me in the pursuit of this project than the members of my family. I would like to thank my parents, whose love and guidance are with me in whatever I pursue. They are the ultimate role models.

Most importantly, I wish to thank my loving and supportive wife Suma HR and my wonderful daughter Ramya C who provide unending inspiration. Last and not least: I beg forgiveness of all those who have been with me over the course of the years and whose names I have failed to mention & quote.

ABOUT THE AUTHOR

With a strong foundation in Electronic Science, garnered through a Master's degree from Bangalore University, and a Bachelor's in PME from Kalpatharu Science College, Chidananda brings a unique perspective to the realm of database management. Currently serving as the Chief Delivery Officer at Ahana, he has been instrumental in shaping the organization's database landscape since 2008. A seasoned professional with a proven track record, Chidananda has held key positions within Ahana, consistently driving operational excellence and delivering exceptional results.

Chidananda's deep understanding of Sybase ASE, coupled with a passion for sharing knowledge, makes him an ideal author for this comprehensive guide. Through years of hands-on experience and a commitment to staying at the forefront of technological advancements, he has developed a profound expertise in database management and performance optimization. This book is a culmination of [his/her/their] extensive knowledge and practical insights, designed to empower readers with the skills and understanding needed to master Sybase ASE.

INTRODUCTION

Introductory Content: The Enduring Relevance of Sybase ASE

Why a Book on Sybase ASE in 2023?

In an era dominated by cloud-native databases and the rapid evolution of database technology, the decision to write a book on Sybase Adaptive Server Enterprise (ASE) might seem counterintuitive. After all, Sybase, once a dominant force in the database landscape, was acquired by SAP in 2010, and its future under the SAP umbrella has been marked by uncertainty.

Yet, the reality is that Sybase ASE continues to power critical applications in many organizations worldwide. Its robust architecture, high performance, and proven reliability have ensured its longevity. This book is a testament to the enduring value of this database platform.

A Legacy of Innovation

Sybase, founded in 1984, was a pioneer in the relational database management system (RDBMS) space. Its flagship product, Sybase SQL Server (later renamed Adaptive Server Enterprise), was among the first commercial RDBMS offerings, setting the stage for the database industry as we know it today. ASE's early adoption by high-performance computing and financial institutions solidified its reputation for speed, reliability, and scalability.

ASE 16.0: The Latest Chapter

Despite the challenges and uncertainties surrounding its future, Sybase ASE has continued to evolve. The release of ASE 16.0 marked a significant milestone, introducing new features and enhancements that address the needs of modern enterprise applications. While it may not boast the same level of innovation as some of its newer competitors, ASE 16.0 remains a powerful and capable database platform.

The Enduring Need

While many organizations have embarked on database modernization initiatives, the transition process is often complex and time-consuming. For those with large, mission-critical applications built on Sybase ASE, migration may not be a feasible option in the short term. These organizations continue to rely on ASE for its stability, performance, and the deep expertise of their database teams.

Moreover, there is a substantial pool of database professionals who have built their careers around Sybase ASE. Their knowledge and experience are invaluable assets to their organizations. This book is designed to serve as a comprehensive resource for these professionals, helping them to maximize the value of their Sybase investments.

In conclusion, while the future of Sybase ASE may be uncertain, its present-day relevance cannot be denied. This book aims to equip database administrators and developers with the knowledge and skills necessary to effectively manage and optimize Sybase ASE systems, ensuring business continuity and success.

While the database landscape is rapidly evolving, the need for comprehensive resources on legacy systems like Sybase ASE remains critical. This book aims to bridge the gap by providing essential

knowledge and practical guidance to database professionals working with this robust and reliable platform.

TABLE OF CONTENTS

CHAPTER – 1
FUNCTIONALITY OF SYSTEM DATABASES AND ARCHITECTURAL OVERVIEW

OVERVIEW

The ASE instance is nothing but a process running on the operating system. The ASE server has its own memory, its own group of databases and background process. So the adaptive server can be thought of as a combination of an instance and a group of databases. When we say an instance, it is a combination of a shared memory structure and a background process.

The memory components and the functionality of the system database will be explained in the following sections.

Figure 1 represents the memory components and databases of adaptive server.

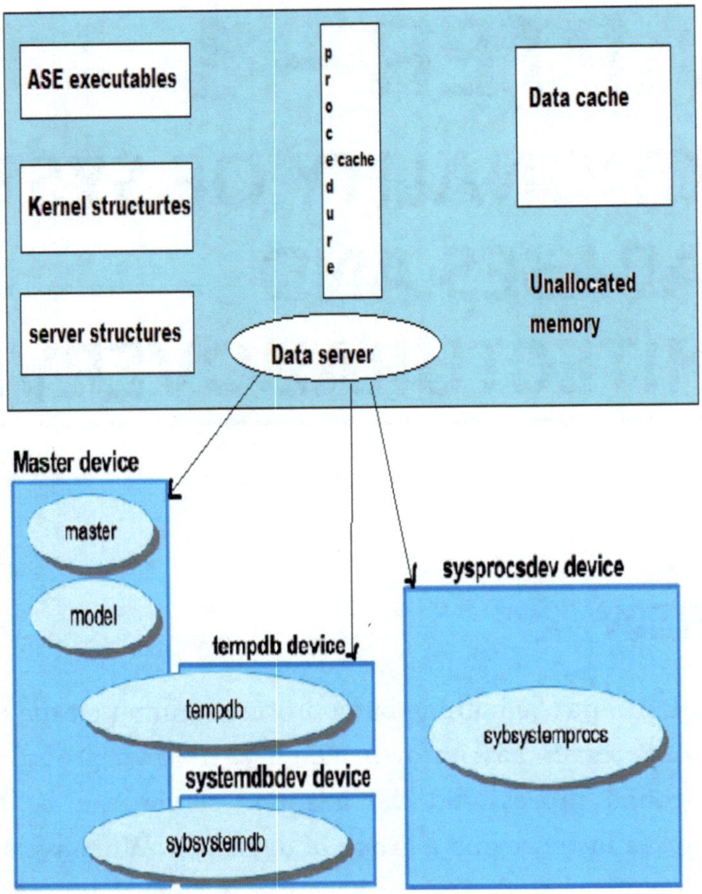

SYSTEM DATABASES AND THEIR FUNCTIONALITY

ASE has five system databases namely-

- master
- model
- tempdb
- sybsystemdb

- sybsystemprocs

Master database

The master database is created on master device, and the default size of the master database is 13MB for a 2K page server. The master database can be viewed as a repository which stores meta data information. In Sybase ASE the system related meta data information is stored in the form of system tables.

The master database is a repository which contains server wide information which is critical for the functioning of the adaptive server.

For example, the master database has information about all the user databases and their associated devices. That means whenever a new database is created all the attributes of the new database is stored in the master database. Similarly, whenever a new login is created the attributes of the new login is stored in the master databases.

The following table shows a few important system tables found in the master database and the information stored in them.

SYSTEM TABLE	INFORMATION
sysdatabases	Attributes of databases
sysdevices	Disks and tapes mounted on the system
sysusages	Space allocated to each device
syslogins	Attributes of a user account
syssrvroles	Server wide roles
sysloginroles	Roles assigned to the logins
sysconfigures	Server wide configuration information
syscharsets	Character sets
sysprocesses	Active processes information
sysengine	ASE engines which are online

It is recommended not to create objects in master database. The master database must be regularly backed up to protect against damaged database.

Run the following query to list the system tables in master -

```
>select name from master..sysobjects
>where type = 'S'
>go
```

Model database

Model database is built on the master device and the size of the model database is 3MB. The model database is used as a template for creating a new database. The purpose of using model database is to copy the system tables to the newly created database.These system tables are needed to store database specific information. You can modify the model database to customize the structure of newly created database.So that the new database inherits the properties of model.

For example, you can create new user defined datatypes, rules or defaults. You can create users who are required to access all the databases of the adaptive server.

The model database cannot be larger than the tempdb.

Every time you customize and make changes in model database, it is recommended to take a backup of model using dump database.

Tempdb database

The srvbuild utility builds the tempdb database on master device and on tempdbdev device. (Version 15.0 and prior to it, the tempdb was built only on master)

The size of tempdb is 104MB. 4MB of space is allocated on master database and 100MB is allocated on tempdbdev.

Tempdb is a temporary database which is used by the user as well as by the system processes. The user can create a session specific temporary table in the tempdb. The system uses the temdb to store intermediate results of query which performs a sort operation. As the sort area in memory is insufficient, the intermediate results are pushed to tempdb. Queries with *order by, group by, having by* clause, crease index statement, join statements, union operator, etc extensively use tempdb.

Sybase allows creating and managing multiple temporary databases.

Sybsystemdb database

The subsystemdb database is built on master device as well as systemdbdev. The size of subsystemdb is 6MB. 3MB of space is allocated on master device and 3MB of space is allocated on systembdev.

The subsystemdb database is used to store information about distributed transactions. It provides transaction co-ordination services which is passed to remote servers. The information about the remote servers is stored in the syscoordination system table.

Subsystemprocs database

The subsystemprocs database is built on sysprocsdev device. The size of the sybsystemprocs database is 172MB. The system stored procedures are stored in the subsystemprocs database. Whenever the system stored procedure is executed ASE looks for the procedure in multiple locations. First it checks in the current database, then it checks in the subsystemprocs database and finally in master database.

In order to change permissions on system stored procedures, the permissions are to be modified in subsystemprocs database.

System Tables in all the Databases

As discussed, using the model database as a template, some system tables are copied into the newly created database. That means a new database is created with system tables which are used to store metadata information pertaining to the database.

For example, when a table, view or a stored procedure is created, the object information is stored in sysobject systemtable. When a database user is created, the information is stored in sysusers system table.

The following table shows a few important system tables which are found in all the databases.

SYSTEM TABLE	INFORMATION
sysobjects	Information about a table, view or a stored procedure.
sysusers	Information about database users.
sysprocedures	The query tree of a stored procedure.
syscomments	Text of a stored procedure , view.
sysattributes	Information abut object attribute definition
sysdepends	Information about dependent objects.
sysindexes	Information about table and its associated indexes.
syscolumns	Information about columns of a table, view or parameters of a stored procedure.
sysusermessages	Stores user created messages.
sysalternates	Mapping for each aliased user.
systabstats	Contains basic statistics for tables and indexes.
sysstatistics	Stores statistics about indexed column.
sysprotects	Information about user permission.
syslogs	Transaction log.
syspartitions	Information about partitioned table.
sysroles	Mapping between server wide roles and the database.
sysreferences	Information about referential integrity constraint of a table declared on a table.
syssegment	Information about each segement.

ASE ARCHITECTURE

The subsequent section will give a description of ASE Architecture. We shall understand the ASE architecture by outlining about-

- processes
- shared memory components
- network

Processes

Every ASE server which is running on a host machine will involve at least one process at the operating system level and it is called as dataserver process.

A single server instance may consist of at least one or more than one dataserver processes running at the operating system level, and they are called *Engines.*

An engine may be defined as an instance of an Adaptive server executable running on a particular CPU. Engines are peers which co-exist, co-operate and communicate with each other in the shared memory.

Using *showserver* utility you could see the active dataserver processes related to ASE server. Also enter the following command to list the active dataserver processes.

$ Ps -ef|grep dataserver

ASE invokes only dataserver process at the operating system and as other processes are internal threads created by ASE and they are invisible at the operating system level.

Path of the data server binary:
$SYBASE/$SYBASE_ASE/bin

Execute the stored procedure **sp_who** to list out the active processes.

Memory Components

The memory components of ASE are

- ASE Executable
- Kernel and server structures
- Procedure cache
- Data cache

ASE Executable

The ASE Executable uses run time memory and this memory is used by Adaptive server for non-configurable data structures.

Kernel and Server Structures

The kernel and server structures together constitutes metadata cache. The metadata cache is a reserved space of memory which is used for tracking information on databases, indexes, objects. That means whenever the server accesses an object, index or opens a database, it needs to gather information from the appropriate system tables.

Frequently reading this information from the disk is expensive and it reduces performance. Hence, this meta data information is stored in the kernel and server structures. This avoids reading the meta data from disk. This server structure component of memory is configurable.

Procedure Cache

The procedure cache is a portion of configurable Adaptive server memory which stores the query plan currently used by the server. The procedure cache is used by the server while executing stored procedures. This avoids reading the abstract plan from the disk. If the query plan is not found in procedure cache, the abstract plan is recompiled to create a copy of the query plan.This is expensive and decreases the performance.

The server applies LRU algorithm to flush out the query plan, i.e, the most recently used query plans are retained in the procedure cache and least frequently used pages are flushed from the cache. This efficiently keeps the requested pages in memory.

The default size of the procedure cache is 7000 pages.

Data cache

The data cache is a large component of memory which holds data pages that have been accessed. When the user needs to read, modify the data in the table, first the pages are read into the data cache. Then the respective data pages are processed.

If a transaction modifies the data, the modification first happens in the data page and the modified page is called *dirty page*. These dirty pages are written to the respective database during an event caused **checkpoint**.

The checkpoint is a database event which writes the dirty pages to the disk.

Whenever a new datapage is requested and read from the disk into data cache, the server looks for a free buffer. If free buffer are not available, it needs to flush out the dirty buffers to make way for the new page. While aging out the data pages the server applies LRU algorithm to flush less frequently used pages. This process tries to retain the busy pages always in memory.

The data cache also contains index pages and log pages, i.e, the index and log pages are also processed in the data cache.

The server has a data cache namely "Default Data Cache" to process the data, index and log pages server wide. The "Default Data Cache" must always exist and the memory for the "Default Data Cache" cannot be made zero.

Sybase allows to exclusively create data caches called *named cache* (discussed later).

Network

When the adaptive server is started, it also starts a listener process to listen for incoming connections on one or more TCP ports. The name of the server is listed in the file called interfaces. The ASE server reads the interfaces file to get the service name and port number. Then the listener service is started in listed port number. If the adaptive server is not able to start the listener services, the dataserver process will not run.

Boot Process

The adaptive server is started using the *startserver* utility. The startserver command has to be run from the path **$SYBASE/$SYBASE_ASE/install.**

To start the server enter the following command.

$ startserver -f RUN<server_name>

The startserver utility executes the RUN_<server_name> file specified in the command line. The **RUN_<server_name>** script in turn calls the dataserver executable with several other parameters listed in the file. Once the memory is available, the server initializes the master device, then other devices. The next sequence is to bring up the system and user databases. Finally the TCP port is opened and the server is ready to accept incoming client connections.

CHAPTER – 2
ADAPTIVE SERVER INSTALLATION

OVERVIEW

One must note that the Adaptive server is designed to run on heterogeneous platforms. ASE can run on Windows, Linux, Unix, Solaris and other operating systems. Even though the server installation on all the platforms has many common things, the installation procedure is slightly different on each platform.

The installation of Adaptive servers needs a certain amount of planning. The most basic things we need to address are-

- Review the hardware and system requirements
- License Requirements
- Selecting appropriate directory path
- Virtual page size for the adaptive server
- Whether to choose partitions or file system devices
- Initial size of the master device
- Whether to install and enable auditing
- Selection of sort order and character set

SYSTEM REQUIREMENTS

This table lists the operating system kernel version, patch requirements, hardware and minimum RAM requirements for installation of Sybase ASE version 15.7

<table>
<tr><th>Operating System</th><th>Kernel Version</th><th>Library Requirements</th><th>Hardware</th><th>Ram Requirement</th></tr>
<tr><td>Red Hat Enterprise Linux 5.0 update: 5</td><td>kernel-2.6.18-53.1.13.el5</td><td rowspan="2">openmotif-2.3.1-2.el5
libXp-1.0.0-8.1.el5
libXt-1.0.2-3.1.fc6
libXtst-1.0.1-3.1
libXmu-1.0.2-5
libXext-1.0.1-2.1
libSM-1.0.1-3.1
libICE-1.0.1-2.1
libX11-1.0.3-9.el5</td><td>Intel Xeon AMD Opteron systems
IBM pSeries Server with POWER5 CPU systems</td><td>512MB</td></tr>
<tr><td>SuSE Linux Enterprise Server (SLES) 11</td><td>kernel-smp-2.6.16.21-0.8</td><td>Intel Xeon AMD Opteron systems
IBM pSeries Server with POWER5 CPU systems</td><td>512MB</td></tr>
</table>

To list the operating system version level, enter-

```
uname -a
```

and to list the packages, enter-

```
rpm -qa
```

PRE INSTALLATION PROCEDURE

In order to maintain consistent ownership and privileges for all files and directories, sybase recommends to create a user by name “sybase”

To create a primary group by name “sybase”, enter-

```
#groupadd sybase
```

To create a user by name "sybase" enter-

```
#useradd -g sybase -d/sybase -m sybase
```

In the above example a user by name sybase is created with home directory being /sybase.

Set the password for the new user

```
#passwd sybase
```

Enter the password *******

Setting the operating system shared memory:

Shared memory of the operating system is used by multiple processes to pass data between the processes. This avoids maintaining redundant copy of the data. The shared memory is required by Adaptive server and backup server processes. The adaptive server allocates shared memory at start up. If sufficient shared memory is not available the server does not start.

To set the shared memory, edit the sysctl.conf file and make an entry for the kernel.shmmax parameter

Example: `vi /etc/sysctl.conf`

```
kernel.shmmax=68719476736
```

In this example shared memory is set to 64GB.

The above tasks are to be performed as a root user.

To start the installer, make sure that you have required operating system patches for the Java Runtime Environment Version 6.

ASE Installation

ASE installation should be performed by connecting to the server as a "sybase" user. The installer suit creates a target directory and all the selected products are unloaded into that directory.

Step 1: Once the ASE software is downloaded, extract the contents into the destination directory.

```
# tar -xvf <file_name>.tar
```

Step 2: Start the installer in GUI mode by entering-

```
./setup -is:javahome JVM
```

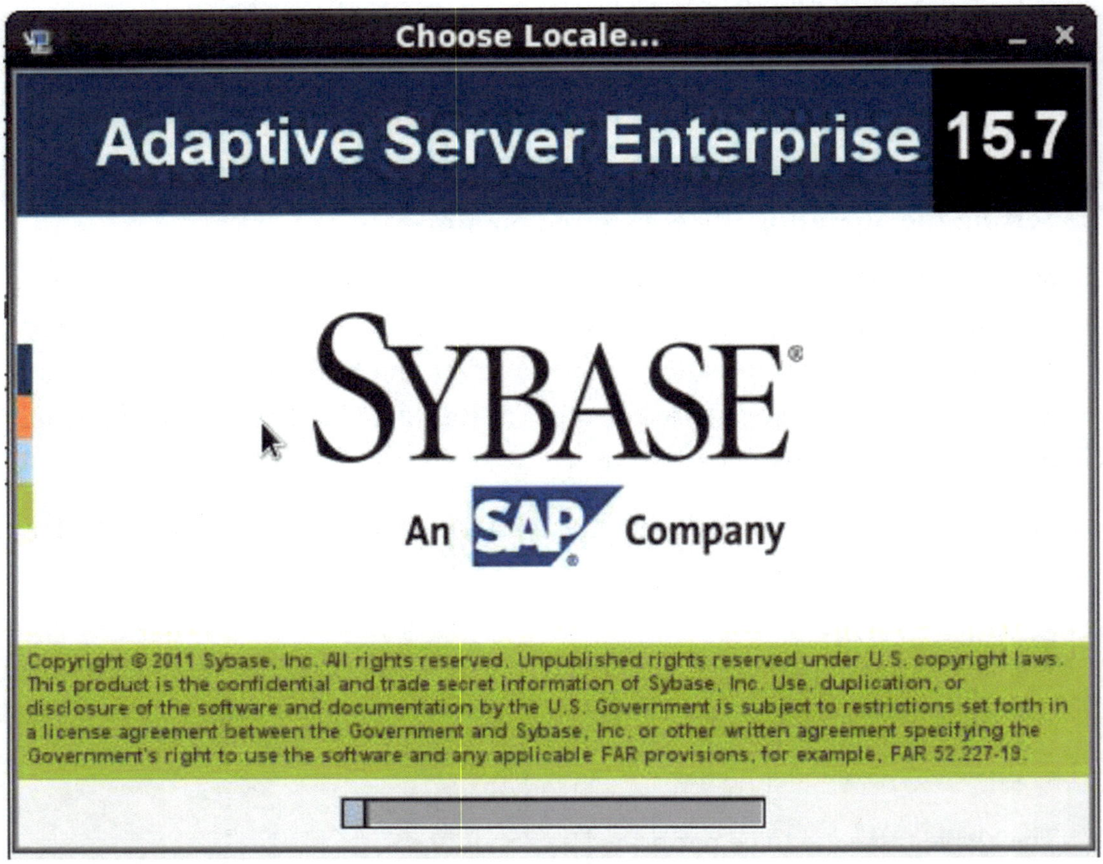

Step 3: Choose the target directory for software installation or accept the default target directory and proceed.

Step 4: The installer allows you to choose any one of the four types product suit, namely-

- Typical: Only English language module is installed and other language modules are not installed.
- Full: All the product features are installed.
- Custom: Products and features will be displayed on the selection window. Select the products to install and proceed.

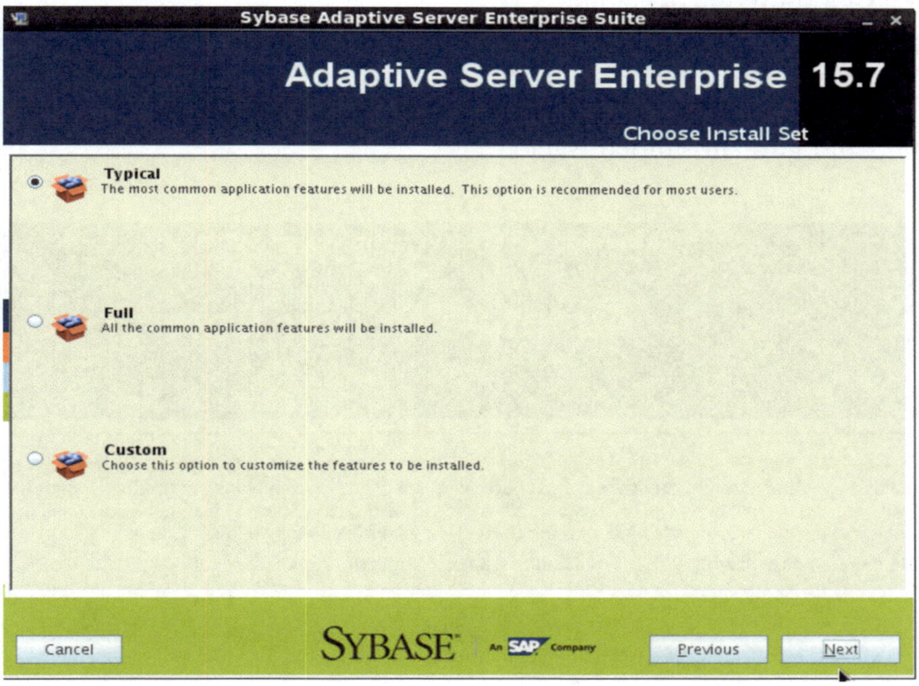

Step 5: Choose the appropriate product license needed. Your choices would be

- Adaptive server Enterprise for evaluation
- Adaptive server enterprise Developer Edition
- Adaptive server enterprise Express Edition

Copy the contents of the license file and process with the installation.

Step 6 (optional)**:** Provide the SMTP server host name, port number, email address information and proceed.

Configuring the Adaptive server

Based on the products installed, the installer suit will prompt you to configure the following new servers.

- Adaptive Server
- Backup Server
- XP Server
- Configure Job Scheduler
- Enable Self Management
- Configure Web Services
- Configure an Unified Agent

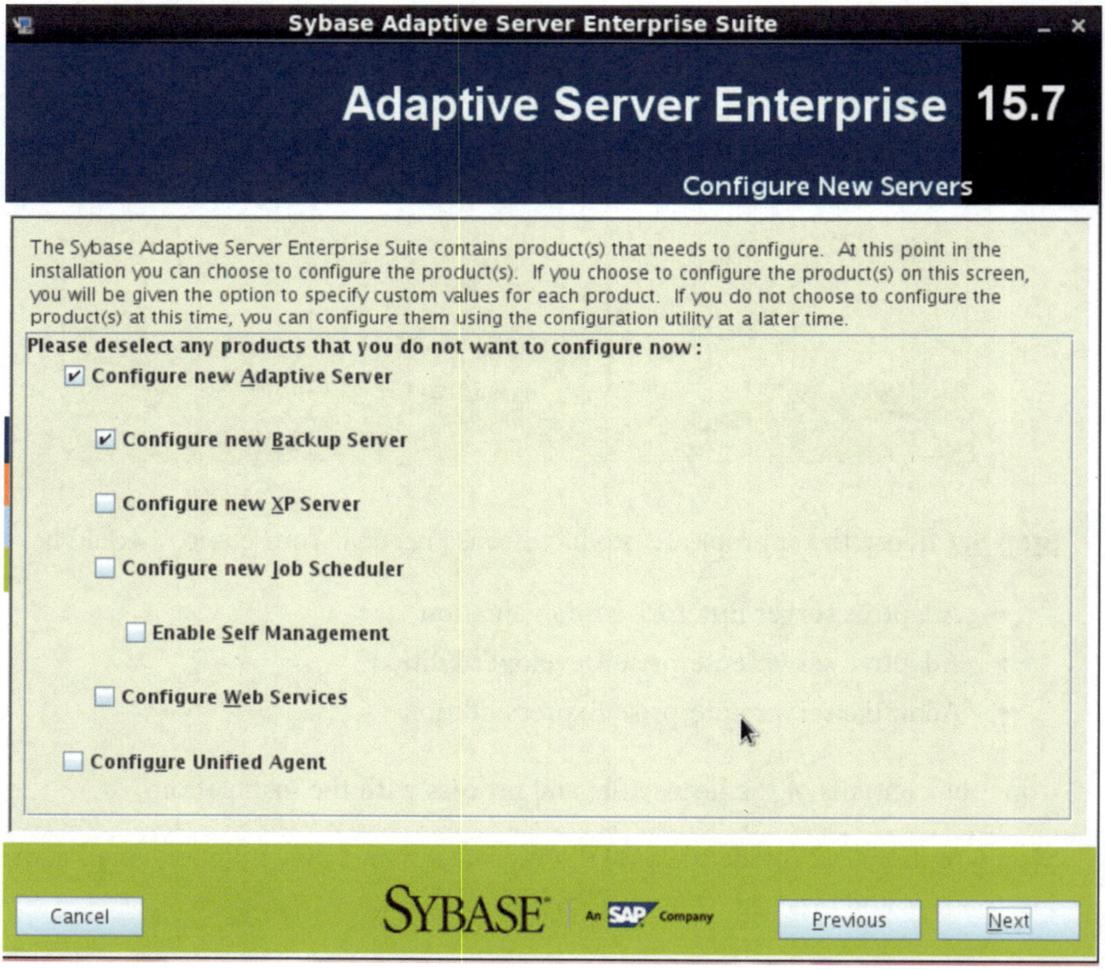

In this installation procedure, let us configure the Adaptive server. To configure the Adaptive server, we need to enter the server name, port number, name and location of the error log. If not chosen, the Adaptive server will use the hostname as the default server name. Let us build an Adaptive server by the name TEST.

Application Type:

Default application type is mixed, meaning both OLTP and DSS. Other options are-

OLTP – Online Transaction processing
DSS- Decision Support System

Choose default and proceed.

Page Size:

The default page size from Sybase ASE version 15.7 is 4K. Note that if you are planning to load the database from a backup, then it is important to choose the page size to match database dump. The page size options available are 2K, 4K, 8K, 16K.

Selecting a lower page size is suitable for OLTP applications. Because the server can cache more number of pages in the data cache memory, Random updates are possible in the data cache memory. This improves data cache hit ratio.

However, in the read intensive DSS applications selecting a large page size is suitable. A larger page size will allow more number of rows to be stored per page. It results in less number of physical reads which improves performance.

Character Set and Sort order:

Adaptive server includes the character set definition files and sort order definition files required for data processing in a majority of languages in Europe, Latin America, Asia and Middle East. By default, the installer chooses native character set of the platform operating system as the servers default character set.

The sort order defines how the server will order storage bytes, how it compares the values in queries and how the query results are ordered the request sorting. The default sort order is binary which stores the information in ASCII numeric order.

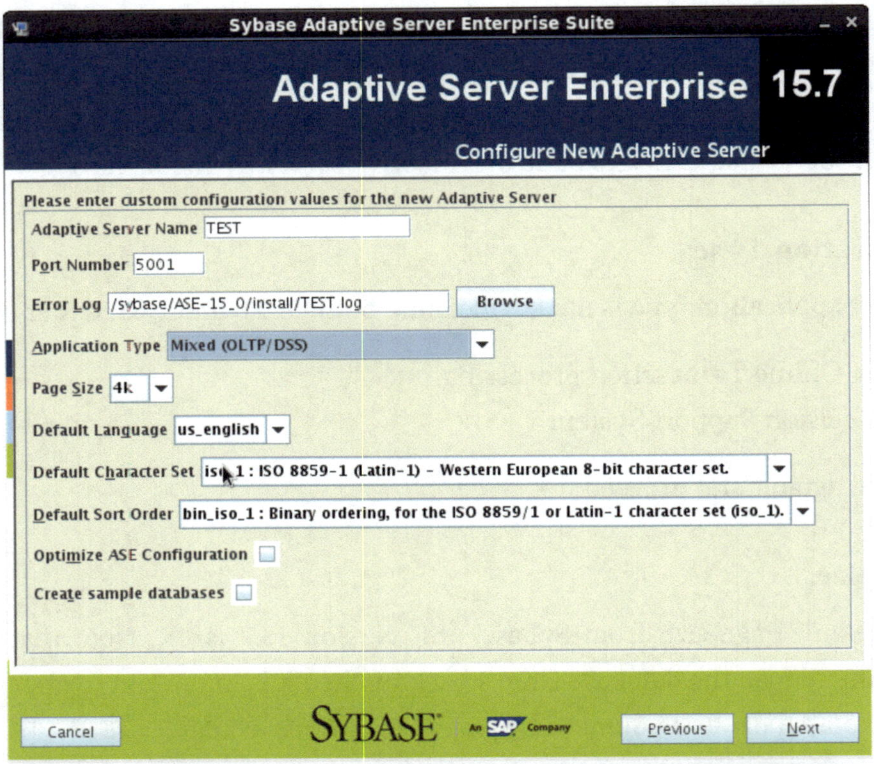
Sybase Adaptive Server Enterprise Suite
Adaptive Server Enterprise 15.7
Configure New Adaptive Server
Please enter custom configuration values for the new Adaptive Server
Adaptive Server Name TEST
Port Number 5001
Error Log /sybase/ASE-15_0/install/TEST.log
Browse
Application Type Mixed (OLTP/DSS)
Page Size 4k
Default Language us_english
Default Character Set iso_1 : ISO 8859-1 (Latin-1) - Western European 8-bit character set.
Default Sort Order bin_iso_1 : Binary ordering, for the ISO 8859/1 or Latin-1 character set (iso_1).
Optimize ASE Configuration
Create sample databases
Cancel
SYBASE
An SAP Company
Previous
Next

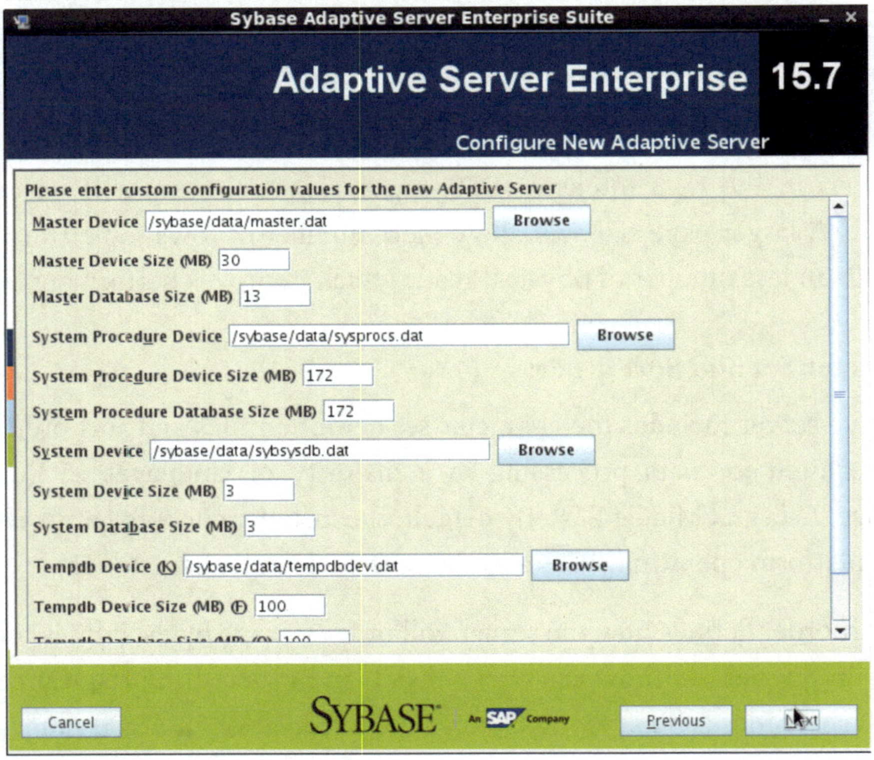
Sybase Adaptive Server Enterprise Suite
Adaptive Server Enterprise 15.7
Configure New Adaptive Server
Please enter custom configuration values for the new Adaptive Server
Master Device /sybase/data/master.dat
Browse
Master Device Size (MB) 30
Master Database Size (MB) 13
System Procedure Device /sybase/data/sysprocs.dat
Browse
System Procedure Device Size (MB) 172
System Procedure Database Size (MB) 172
System Device /sybase/data/sybsysdb.dat
Browse
System Device Size (MB) 3
System Database Size (MB) 3
Tempdb Device (K) /sybase/data/tempdbdev.dat
Browse
Tempdb Device Size (MB) (F) 100
Cancel
SYBASE
An SAP Company
Previous
Next

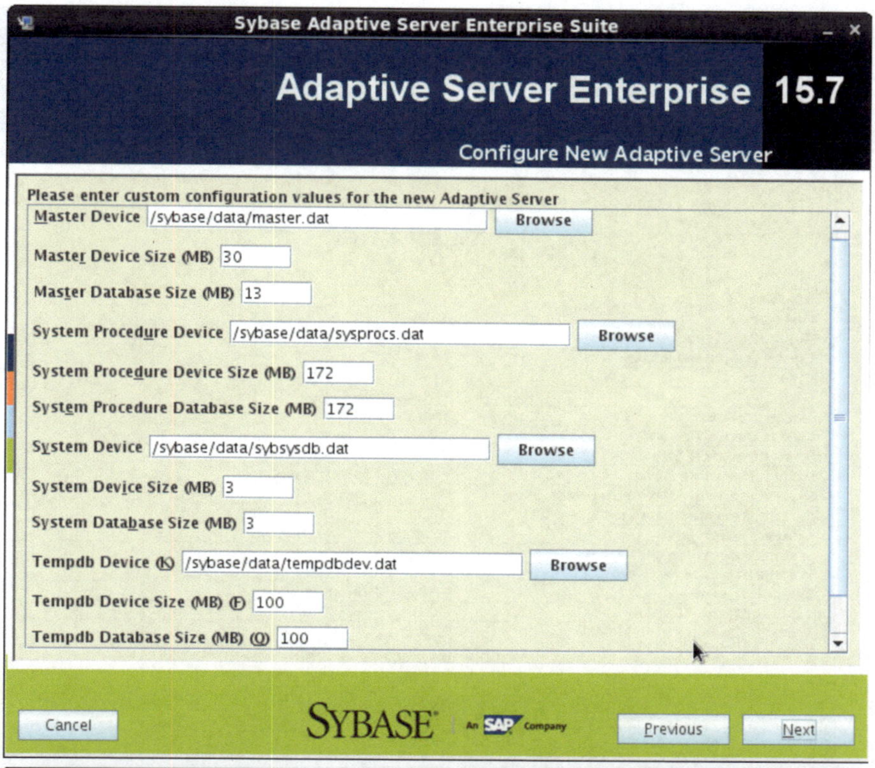
Sybase Adaptive Server Enterprise Suite
Adaptive Server Enterprise 15.7
Configure New Adaptive Server
Please enter custom configuration values for the new Adaptive Server
Master Device /sybase/data/master.dat
Browse
Master Device Size (MB) 30
Master Database Size (MB) 13
System Procedure Device /sybase/data/sysprocs.dat
Browse
System Procedure Device Size (MB) 172
System Procedure Database Size (MB) 172
System Device /sybase/data/sybsysdb.dat
Browse
System Device Size (MB) 3
System Database Size (MB) 3
Tempdb Device (K) /sybase/data/tempdbdev.dat
Browse
Tempdb Device Size (MB) (F) 100
Tempdb Database Size (MB) (Q) 100
Cancel
SYBASE
An SAP Company
Previous
Next

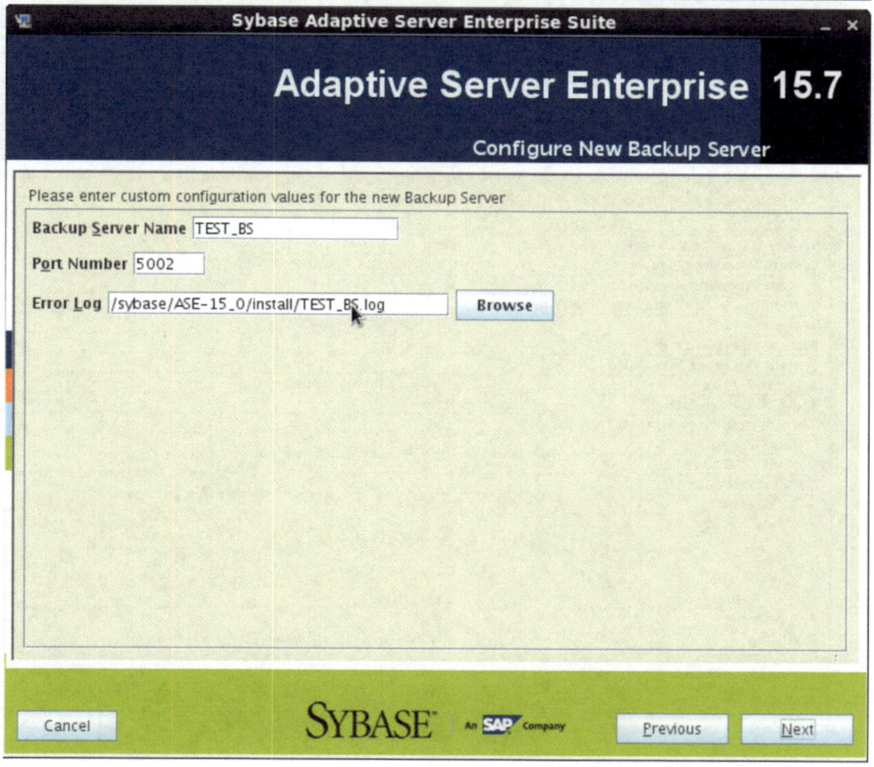
Sybase Adaptive Server Enterprise Suite
Adaptive Server Enterprise 15.7
Configure New Backup Server
Please enter custom configuration values for the new Backup Server
Backup Server Name TEST_BS
Port Number 5002
Error Log /sybase/ASE-15_0/install/TEST_BS.log
Browse
Cancel
SYBASE
An SAP Company
Previous
Next

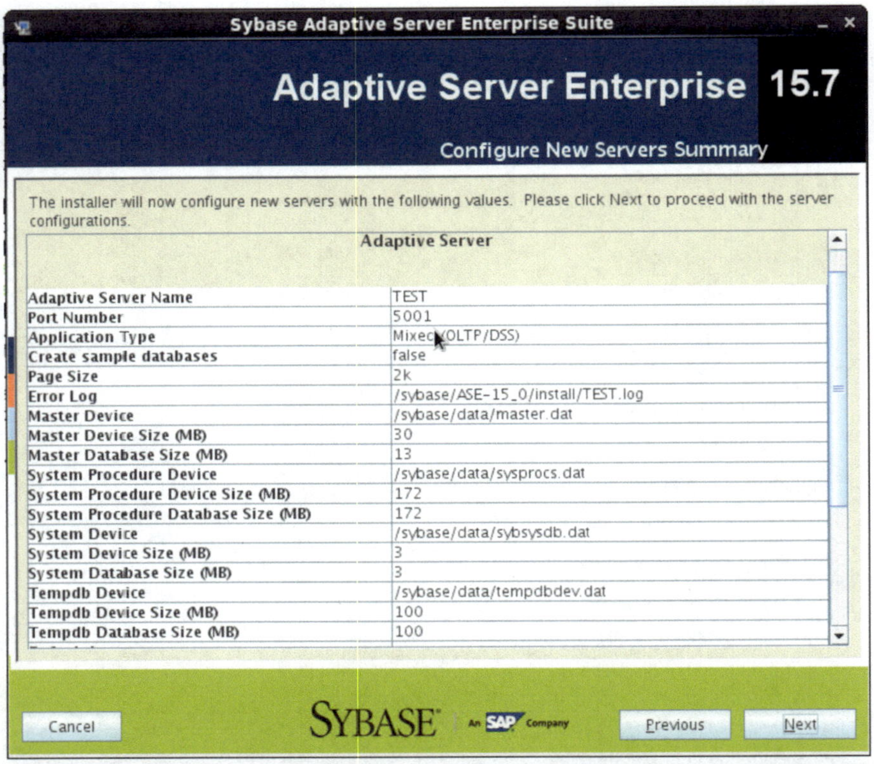
Sybase Adaptive Server Enterprise Suite
Adaptive Server Enterprise 15.7
Configure New Servers Summary
The installer will now configure new servers with the following values. Please click Next to proceed with the server configurations.
Adaptive Server
Adaptive Server Name TEST
Port Number 5001
Application Type Mixed(OLTP/DSS)
Create sample databases false
Page Size 2k
Error Log /sybase/ASE-15_0/install/TEST.log
Master Device /sybase/data/master.dat
Master Device Size (MB) 30
Master Database Size (MB) 13
System Procedure Device /sybase/data/sysprocs.dat
System Procedure Device Size (MB) 172
System Procedure Database Size (MB) 172
System Device /sybase/data/sybsysdb.dat
System Device Size (MB) 3
System Database Size (MB) 3
Tempdb Device /sybase/data/tempdbdev.dat
Tempdb Device Size (MB) 100
Tempdb Database Size (MB) 100
Cancel
SYBASE
An SAP Company
Previous
Next

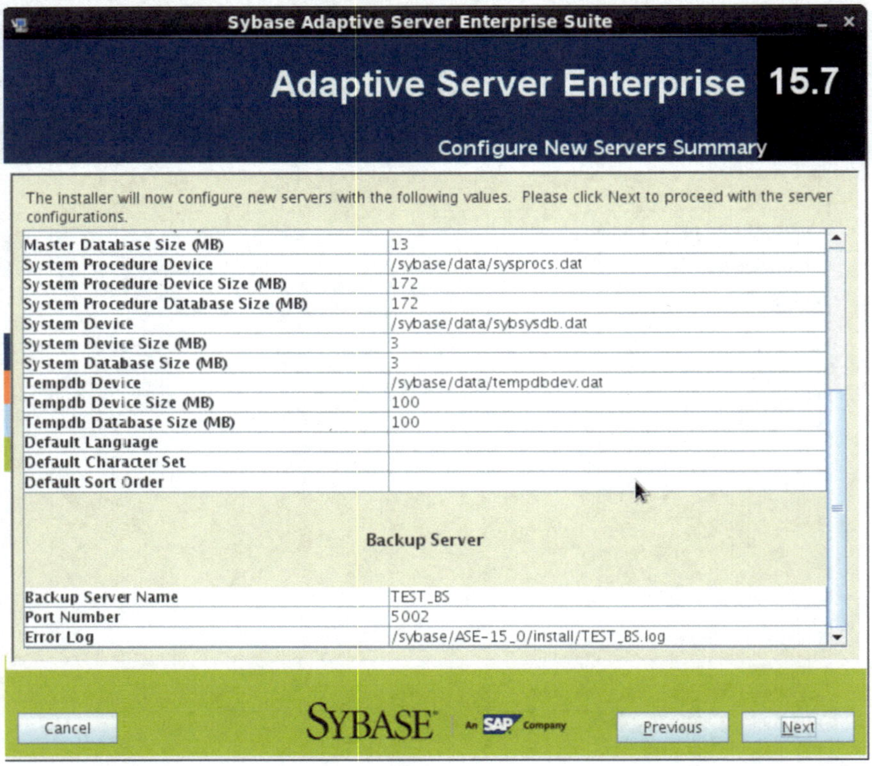
Sybase Adaptive Server Enterprise Suite
Adaptive Server Enterprise 15.7
Configure New Servers Summary
The installer will now configure new servers with the following values. Please click Next to proceed with the server configurations.
Master Database Size (MB) 13
System Procedure Device /sybase/data/sysprocs.dat
System Procedure Device Size (MB) 172
System Procedure Database Size (MB) 172
System Device /sybase/data/sybsysdb.dat
System Device Size (MB) 3
System Database Size (MB) 3
Tempdb Device /sybase/data/tempdbdev.dat
Tempdb Device Size (MB) 100
Tempdb Database Size (MB) 100
Default Language
Default Character Set
Default Sort Order
Backup Server
Backup Server Name TEST_BS
Port Number 5002
Error Log /sybase/ASE-15_0/install/TEST_BS.log
Cancel
SYBASE
An SAP Company
Previous
Next

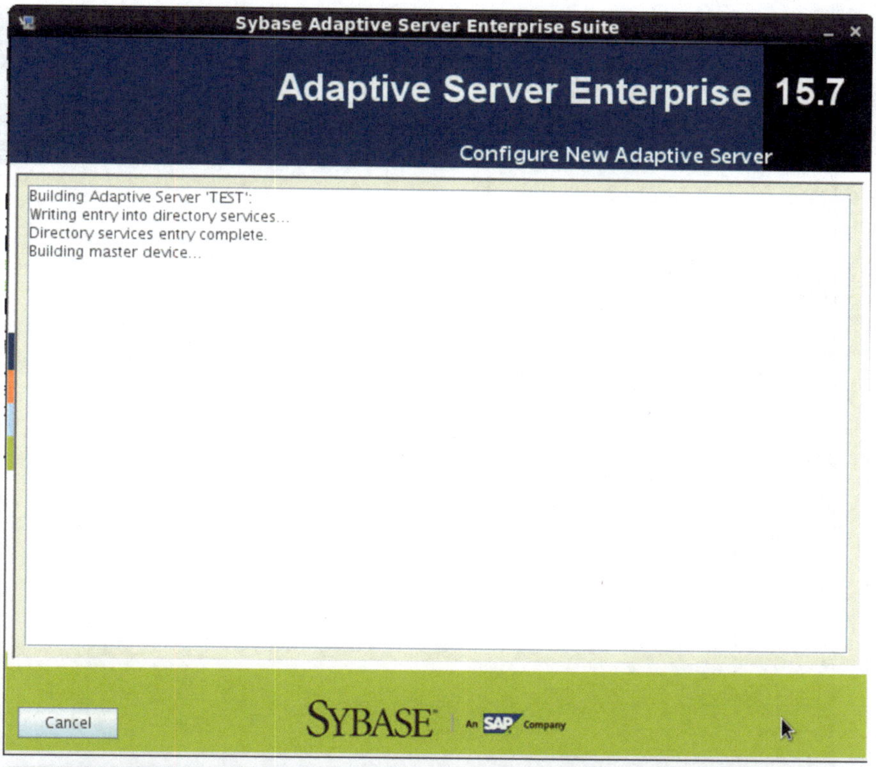
Sybase Adaptive Server Enterprise Suite
Adaptive Server Enterprise 15.7
Configure New Adaptive Server
Building Adaptive Server 'TEST':
Writing entry into directory services...
Directory services entry complete.
Building master device...
Cancel
SYBASE An SAP Company

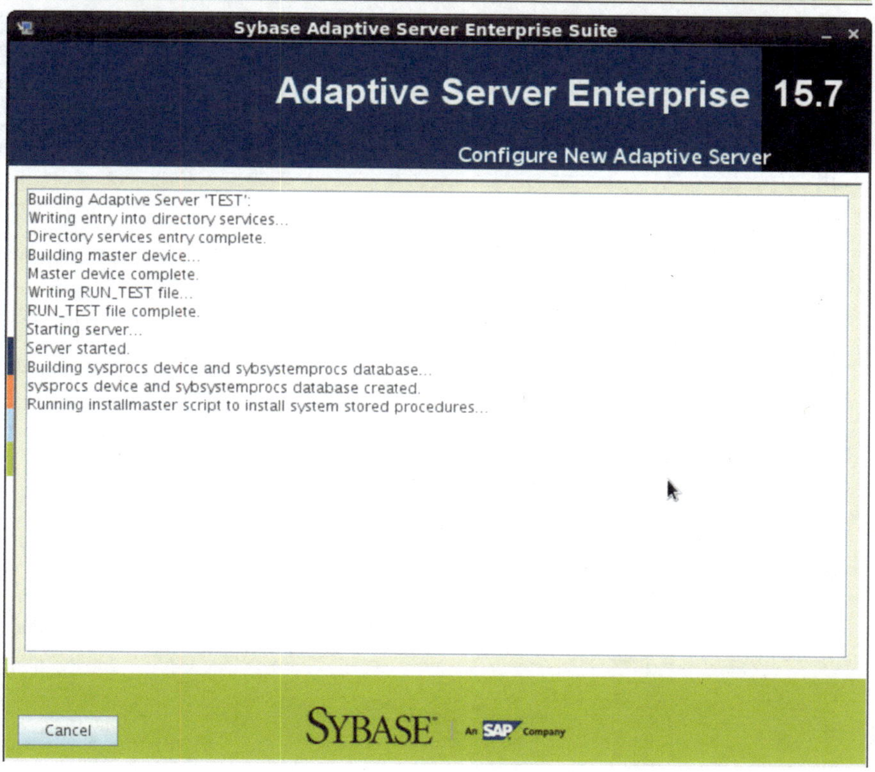
Sybase Adaptive Server Enterprise Suite
Adaptive Server Enterprise 15.7
Configure New Adaptive Server
Building Adaptive Server 'TEST':
Writing entry into directory services...
Directory services entry complete.
Building master device...
Master device complete.
Writing RUN_TEST file...
RUN_TEST file complete.
Starting server...
Server started.
Building sysprocs device and sybsystemprocs database...
sysprocs device and sybsystemprocs database created.
Running installmaster script to install system stored procedures...
Cancel
SYBASE An SAP Company

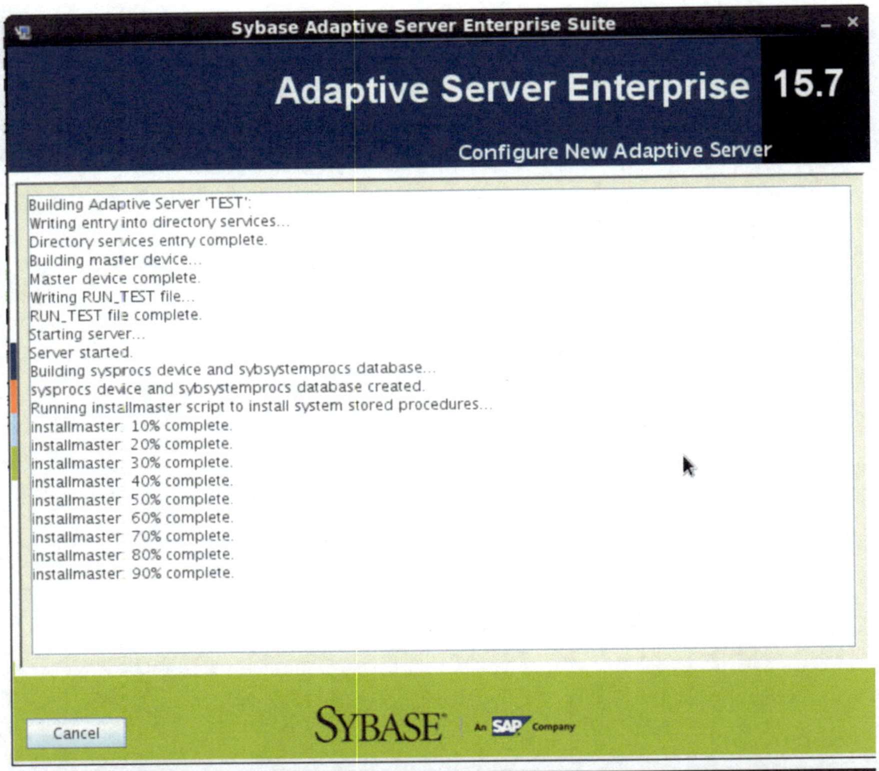
Sybase Adaptive Server Enterprise Suite
Adaptive Server Enterprise 15.7
Configure New Adaptive Server
Building Adaptive Server 'TEST':
Writing entry into directory services...
Directory services entry complete.
Building master device...
Master device complete.
Writing RUN_TEST file...
RUN_TEST file complete.
Starting server...
Server started.
Building sysprocs device and sybsystemprocs database...
sysprocs device and sybsystemprocs database created.
Running installmaster script to install system stored procedures...
installmaster: 10% complete.
installmaster: 20% complete.
installmaster: 30% complete.
installmaster: 40% complete.
installmaster: 50% complete.
installmaster: 60% complete.
installmaster: 70% complete.
installmaster: 80% complete.
installmaster: 90% complete.
Cancel
SYBASE An SAP Company

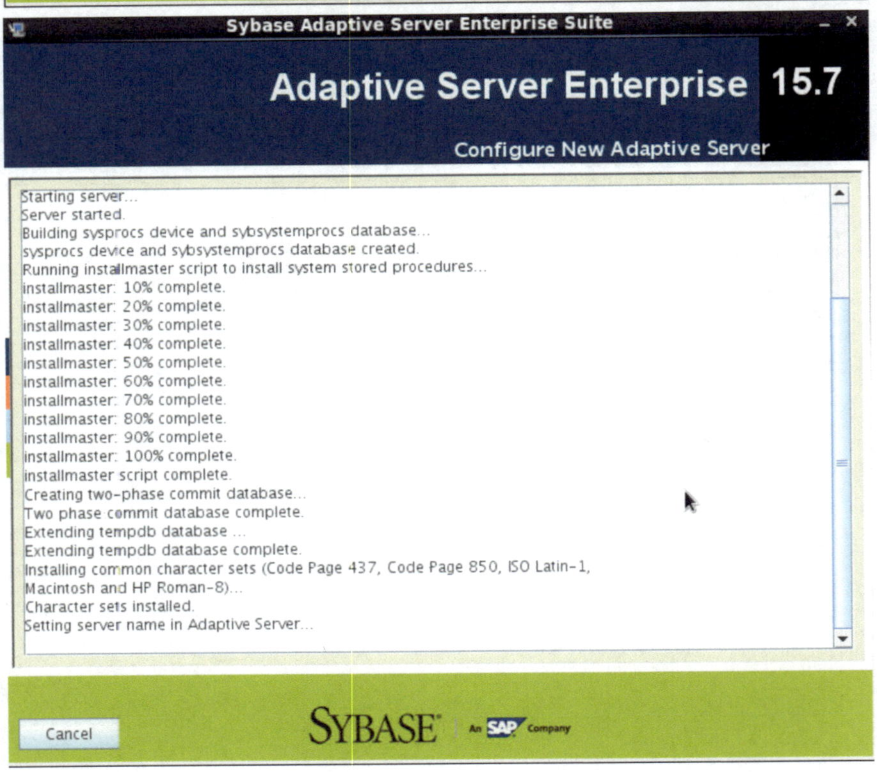
Sybase Adaptive Server Enterprise Suite
Adaptive Server Enterprise 15.7
Configure New Adaptive Server
Starting server...
Server started.
Building sysprocs device and sybsystemprocs database...
sysprocs device and sybsystemprocs database created.
Running installmaster script to install system stored procedures...
installmaster: 10% complete.
installmaster: 20% complete.
installmaster: 30% complete.
installmaster: 40% complete.
installmaster: 50% complete.
installmaster: 60% complete.
installmaster: 70% complete.
installmaster: 80% complete.
installmaster: 90% complete.
installmaster: 100% complete.
installmaster script complete.
Creating two-phase commit database...
Two phase commit database complete.
Extending tempdb database ...
Extending tempdb database complete.
Installing common character sets (Code Page 437, Code Page 850, ISO Latin-1,
Macintosh and HP Roman-8)...
Character sets installed.
Setting server name in Adaptive Server...
Cancel
SYBASE An SAP Company

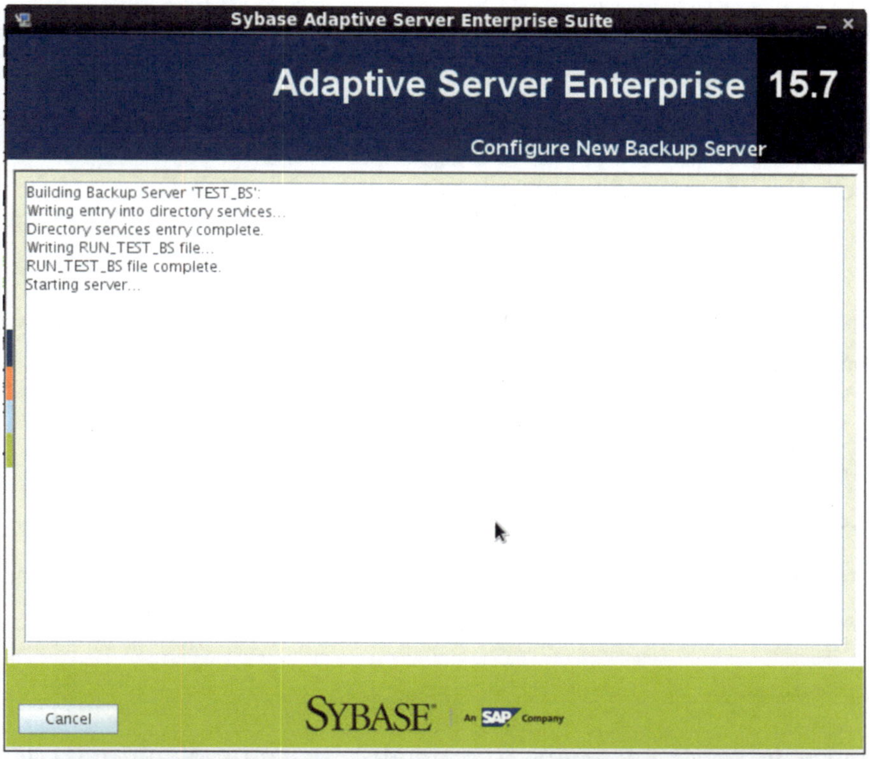
Sybase Adaptive Server Enterprise Suite
Adaptive Server Enterprise 15.7
Configure New Backup Server
Building Backup Server 'TEST_BS':
Writing entry into directory services...
Directory services entry complete.
Writing RUN_TEST_BS file...
RUN_TEST_BS file complete.
Starting server...
Cancel
SYBASE
An SAP Company

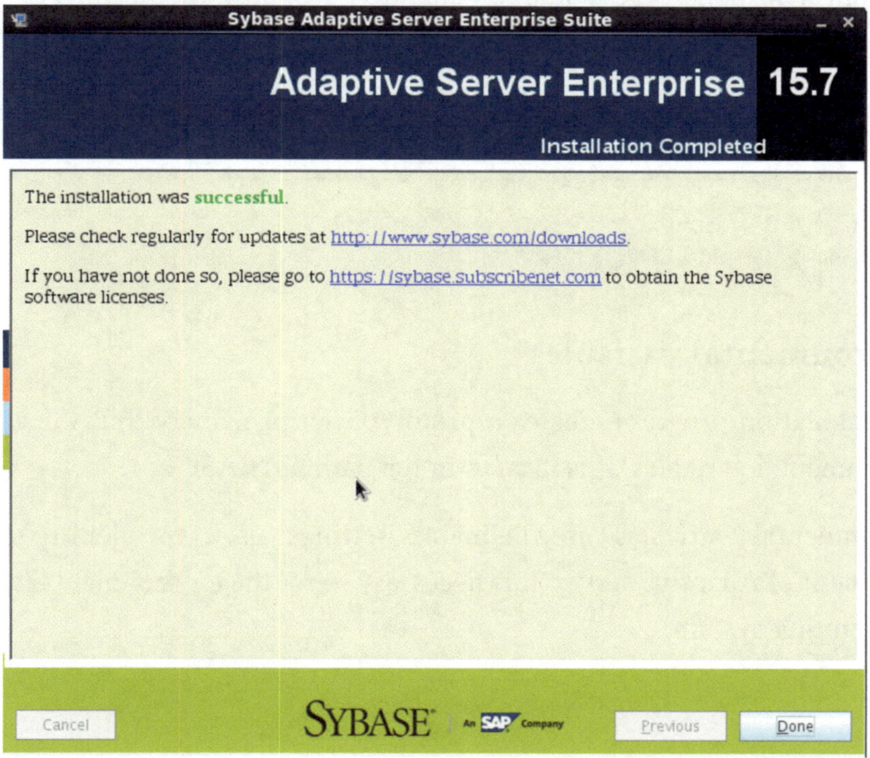
Sybase Adaptive Server Enterprise Suite
Adaptive Server Enterprise 15.7
Installation Completed
The installation was successful.
Please check regularly for updates at http://www.sybase.com/downloads.
If you have not done so, please go to https://sybase.subscribenet.com to obtain the Sybase software licenses.
Cancel
SYBASE
An SAP Company
Previous
Done

The installation is completed with the configuration of the server.

Installing the Adaptive server in the console mode

To choose the command line installation, enter:

```
./setup.bin -i console
```

This starts the installation program. The installation steps are similar to the regular GUI installation.

Unattended, Silent mode installation

If you are performing more than one installation of Adaptive server, we can generate the responses into a response file. Then edit the file to customize the responses.

Use the command

setup.bin -r response_file_name to generate a response file during console or GUI installation.

Then run the following command by specifying the response file.

```
setup.bin -r response_file_name -i silent
-D AGREE_TO_SYNASE_LICENSE=true
-D RUN_SILENT=true
```

Environmental variables

The installation program creates a prototype script namely SYBASE.sh to set the environmental variables. It is located in the path $SYBASE .

Environmental variables are definable settings used to identify appropriate component of Adaptive server .It is necessary to set the environmental variables for the operating system.

Few important environmental variables are listed as follows

Variable	Description
$SYBASE	Sybase installation base directory
$SYBASE_ASE	The sub-directory where the server components of the server are installed
$SYBASE_OCS	The sub-directory where the open client components are installed
$DSQUERY	It represents the name of the default server used by the clients to connect to the Adaptive server
$DSLISTEN	It represents the default name of the Adaptive server used by the startserver utility to start the adaptive server, if the name is not specified in the run server script
$SYBASE_SYSAM	It represents the sub-directory where the Software Asset Manager is located

Once the environment variables are set,

- Verify that the server is running, enter at the command prompt showserver
- Verify the connection to the server using the isql utility

```
isql -U<username> -P<password> -S<servername>
```

The adaptive server creates login called "sa" with null password. It is recommended to change the "sa" password.

To change the sa password enter the following-

```
sp_password null, <new_password>, sa
go
```

To verify the current version enter:

```
select @@version
go
```

To view the databases enter-

```
sp_helpdb
go
```

Note that when we build a 2K page server, the Adaptive server builds the system databases and system devices as mentioned in the following table.

DATABASE	SIZE	DEVICE	SIZE
Master	13MB	Master	30MB
Model	3MB	Sysprocsdev	172MB
Tempdb	104MB	Tempdbdev	100MB
Sybsystemdb	6MB	Systemdbdev	3MB
Sybsystemprocs	172MB		

Interfaces file

Interfaces file is part of Adaptive server Directory services through which we define the server address and port number and connection protocol information

In the UNIX environment the connection descriptor information is stored in the interfaces file and it is located in the base installation directory

In WINDOWS platform the connection descriptor information is stored in the sql.ini file and it is located in the directory %SYBASE\ini directory

The interface file needs to be accessed by each client application to connect to the adaptive server and it is also accessed by the startserver utility in order to start the adaptive server.

The typical interfaces entry is shown below.

TEST

```
master tcp ether localhost 5000
query tcp ether localhost 5000
```

For each services listed in the interfaces file,

The first entry represents the service name.

The master entry represents the hostname and port number which is used by the startserver utility to start the adaptive server

The query entry represents the hostname and port number information used by the clients to connect to the Adaptive server

CHAPTER – 3
CONFIGURATION PARAMETERS AND MEMORY CONFIGURATION

OVERVIEW

As explained in Chapter 2, the RUN_<server_name> executes the dataserver executable and passes various parameters. The parameters passed are:

-d : Specifies the path for initializing the master device on the file
-e : Specifies the path of error log file
-c : Specifies the path of configuration file
-M : Directory for shared memory files
-s : Name of the server

The adaptive server uses the configuration file specified in the RUN_<server_name> script to configure memory and to configure thebehaviour of the Adaptive server

In this chapter we shall understand how the Adaptive server uses configuration file at startup and allocates memory.

THE ADAPTIVE SERVER CONFIGURATION FILE

The configuration file is a ASCII text file, which contains configuration parameters used by the server. The default name of the configuration file is

<server_name>.cfg.

The default path is $SYBASE/$SYBASE_ASE

Configuration parameters are user definable settings which control the behaviour of Adaptive server. When the server is created for first time, the server supplies default values for the configuration parameters. Based on the application needs, the configuration parameters needs to be changed to customize the server behaviour.

Type of configuration parameters

The configuration parameters can be classified as:

Dynamic parameters: When the configuration option is changed using sp_configure system procedure, the changed option is affected immediately and the server need not be restarted.

Static parameters: When the configuration option is changed using sp_configure system procedure, the Adaptive server needs to be restarted for the value to be effective.

Read Only parameters: The configuration is read only and it cannot be modified.

Example: Total physical memory, total logical memory

Modifying the configuration parameters

The configuration parameters can be changed using the system procedure sp_configure.

For example, `sp_configure "number of user connections"`

```
Parameter Name
        Default             Memory              UsedConfig Value
        Run Value           Unit
        Type
     ---------------------------------------------------
---------
     ---------------------- ---------------------- -----
-------------------
     ------------------------ --------------------------
--------------
     --------------------
number of user connections
                25                  4814                25
                25                  number
        dynamic
(1 row affected)
(return status = 0)
```

The configuration option is changed in the following sequence:

- The server makes a copy of the <server_name>.cfg file and saves the file as <server_name>.000 file.

- Updates the new value to the <server_name>.cfg file.
- If the parameter is dynamic the value will be effective immediately. So in the sp_configure output you could see the run value matching with the configured value.
- If the parameter is static, only the <server_name>.cfg file is updated with the configuration parameter and we need to restart the server for the value to be effective. In this case the run value differs from the configured value before you restart the server.

For example, `sp_configure "default network packet size", 1024`

```
Parameter Name
        Default         Memory Used     Config Value
        Run Value       Unit
        Type
     ---------------------------------------------------
---------
     ---------------------- ---------------------- -----
-------------------
     ------------------------ --------------------------
--------------
     --------------------
default network packet size
                2048            #536            1024
                2048            bytes
        static
(1 row affected)
```

```
Configuration option changed. Since the option is static, Adaptive Server must be rebooted in order for the change to take effect.
```

```
Changing the value of 'default network packet size' does not increase the amount of memory Adaptive Server uses.

(return status = 0)
```

To reset the configuration option to the default settings, enter the following:

```
sp_configure 'parameter_name',0, 'default'
```

sp_configure Subcommands

You can generate a copy of the configuration parameters currently used by the server using the system procedure sp_configure.

The sp_configure system procedure has the following subcommands:

Write – The write option creates a new configuration file which contains all the active values used by the Adaptive server. If this new configuration file is used to start the other server, the behaviour of the two servers will be similar.

Restore – The restore option creates a new configuration file which has most recently configured parameter values which may be either active or inactive. This option is useful if all the copies of the configuration file are lost.

Verify – The verify option performs a validation check on the values specified in the configuration file. This is particularly useful if you have manually edited the configuration file. This prevents you from attempting to start your server with invalid values.

Read – The read option performs validation check on the specified configuration file and passes the values into the server.

To view the information about configuration parameters use the system procedure:

```
sp_helpconfig "parameter name"
```

For example, `sp_helpconfig "max memory"`

```
max memory sets the maximum size of memory, in 2K units,
that ASE can allocate.

Minimum Value Maximum Value Default Value Current Value
Memory Used

Unit Type

     ------------- ------------- ------------- ---------
---- ----------------------

     ---------------------------------- -------------

     40960       2097151 40960   40960   81920

     memory pages(2k)            dynamic

(return status = 0)
```

Configuration file at startup

Each time the adaptive server is restarted the server makes a backup copy of the <server_name>.cfg file. It is called by <server_name>.bak file. If the server is not starting with the current configurations, you can either use <server_name>.000 files or <server_name>.bak file to start the adaptive server.

System tables related to Configuration parameters

sysconfigures– This system table is contained in the master database and it stores the configuration values from the startup time or from the last modification of the parameter value.

Syscurconfigs – This system table is contained in the master database and it stores the configuration values which are currently used by the server.Thesyscurconfig system table information is built dynamically when queried.

MEMORY CONFIGURATIONS

When the ASE instance is started it takes memory from the operating system for its internal buffers and caches and starts the data server process. Basically having more memory for the caches will increase the capability to read and store data form the disk. This improves the server performance.

The memory that is obtained from the operating system is controlled by the configuration parameter "max memory". The default value of "max memory" is platform dependent.

To view the configured value enter:

```
sp_configure 'max memory'
```

```
max memory sets the maximum size of memory, in 2K units,
that ASE can allocate.

Minimum Value Maximum Value Default Value Current Value
Memory Used

              Unit                        Type

     ------------- ------------- ------------- ---------
---- ----------------------

     --------------------------------- --------------

     40960       2097151          40960    40960    81920
     memory pages(2k)             dynamic

(return status = 0)
```

The 'max memory' is a dynamic parameter. More the memory available to the Adaptive server, the better will be the Adaptive server performance.

To allocate memory to the adaptive server, estimate the memory needs of your operating system, and other applications and memory needed by the backup server. Then allocate the remaining available memory to the server using the parameter sp_configure.

Example-

```
sp_configure "max memory", number of pages.
```

Note that there is no performance penalty for allocating maximum amount of memory available to adaptive server.

Regardless of the logical page size, the memory allocation page size is always 2K, i.e, if you build the adaptive server with 8K as logical page size, the memory page allocation is still in terms of 2K pages.

Memory Allocation sequence at startup

The total amount of memory needed to start the server is the sum of memory requirement of metadata cache plus the procedure cache plus the data cache. The sum of all three individual components **should not exceed the max memory.** So max memory is the upper limit within which you can allocate memory to individual components. When the adaptive server is started, the memory requirement is computed based on the e memory dependent configuration parameters. This memory is called as **total logical memory**. You can view the total logical memory using the read only parameter "total logical memory".

For example, sp_configure "total logical memory"

```
Parameter Name
        Default          Memory Used      Config Value
        Run Value        Unit
        Type
     ---------------------------------------------------
---------
     ---------------------- ---------------------- -----
-------------------
     ------------------------ --------------------------
--------------
     --------------------
procedure cache size
                7000              14822              7000
                7000              memory pages(2k)
        dynamic
```

```
(1 row affected)
```

This total logical memory must be less than the max memory. Then the server starts up. If the memory is unavailable, the server cannot start. The memory allocation sequence is:

- A fixed memory is allocated for the non-dynamic memory structures, i.e, ASE Executables.
- Memory is allocated for the kernel structures.
- Memory is allocated for the server structures based on the specification in the configuration file.
- Memory is allocated for the procedure cache and data cache.

The rest of the memory is unallocated memory. Also if there is not sufficient memory to support current configuration, the server will not start.

Memory Allocation behaviour

You can control the memory allocation behaviour by configuring the parameter "allocate max shared memory"

Example: `sp_configure "allocate max shared memory"`

```
Parameter Name
        Default         Memory Used     Config Value
        Run Value       Unit
        Type
     -----------------------------------------------------
---------
     ---------------------- ---------------------- -----
-------------------
     ------------------------ --------------------------
--------------
     --------------------
```

```
allocate max shared memory
                    0                   0                   0
                    0                   switch
          dynamic
(1 row affected)
(return status = 0)
```

The default value is zero. Meaning that the memory allocation is based on the requirements as specified in the configuration file only.

For example, let us consider that the 'total logical memory' needed is 32GB and the max memory parameter is configured for 48GB. When the server starts up it allocates a memory of 32GB. If "allocate max shared memory" is configured to one, then the memory allocation is based on the max memory only. That means irrespective of the current memory demands, the server grabs 48GB from the operating system.

The parameter "Dynamic allocation on demand" controls the dynamic memory allocation. This is explained with an example.

If you have configured "dynamic allocation on demand" parameter to default value 1, then the server allocates the memory on demand basis. Let us say the number of user connection is configured to 2000. Then the logical memory needed would be 2000 multiplied by the amount of memory per user. Now if only 1000 session are established, then the server allocates memory for 1000 users. As the active connections increases then memory is allocated on demand basis. However if the user connections fall down, the memory will not be dynamically released. The acquired memory will only be released during server restart.

If the parameter "dynamic allocation on demand" is configured to non-default value i,e 0, the requested memory is allocated immediately.

Configuring Procedure cache

To view the existing procedure cache size, enter:

```
sp_configure "procedure cache size"

Parameter Name
        Default             Memory Used      Config Value
        Run Value           Unit
        Type
     --------------------------------------------------
---------
     -------------------- -------------------- -----
------------------
     ---------------------- ------------------------
--------------
     -------------------

procedure cache size
                7000            14822           7000
                7000            memory pages(2k)
        dynamic
(1 row affected)
(return status = 0)
```

The default size of the procedure cache is 7000 memory pages. It is to be noted again that regardless of the logical page size, the server always allocates memory pages in terms of 2K. S o the memory allocated is 7000 x 2K, i.e, 14MB.

To configure the procedure cache to a different value, enter:

```
sp_configure "procedure cache size", 16000

Parameter Name

        Default             Memory Used        Config Value
        Run Value           Unit
        Type

     ---------------------------------------------------
---------
     ---------------------- ---------------------- -----
-------------------
     ------------------------ --------------------------
--------------
     --------------------

procedure cache size

                7000                33882               16000

                16000               memory pages(2k)

        dynamic

(1 row affected)
Configuration option changed. ASE need not be rebooted
since the option is
dynamic.
Resulting configuration value and memory use have not
changed from previous
values: new configuration value 16000, previous value
16000.
(return status = 0)
```

Consideration: You can monitor the percentage active usage of the procedure cache size using system procedure sp_monitorconfig.

Example:

```
sp_monitorconfig "procedure cache size"
```

```
Usage information at date and time: Feb 18 2014 5:55PM.
Name                                        Num_freeNum_active
        Pct_actMax_UsedNum_Reuse
     ----------------------------------------------------- --------
--- -----------
     ----------- ----------- -----------
procedure cache size 13336 2664
                 16.65            2985             0
(return status = 0)
```

If the percentage active usage is approaching 100%, consider increasing the procedure cache size. If the memory for procedure cache is not enough, then the server may displace the active memory pages from the procedure cache. This leads to reusing of the abstract query plan and recompile the query plan. This affects performance.

Data cache and named cache configurations

The server reads data page, index page and log page into "default data cache". This data cache must always exist and it cannot be dropped. By default all the database objects are implicitly bound to the "default data cache".

To determine the cache size and other related information, use the system procedure sp_cacheconfig and sp_helpcache.

For example, `sp_cacheconfig "default data cache"`

```
Cache Name                  Status          Type
        Config Value                Run Value
------------------------------------ ------------ -------------
                        -------------
      ----------------------- -----------------------
default data cache                Active             Default
                 1.00 Mb          8.00 Mb
```

```
                                ------------ ------------
                Total           1.00 Mb      8.00 Mb
================================================================
==========
Cache: default data cache, Status: Active, Type: Default
Config Size: 1.00 Mb,      Run Size: 8.00 Mb
Config Replacement: strict LRU, Run Replacement: strict LRU
Config Partition:          1, Run Partition: 1
IO Size         Wash Size                  Config Size
                Run Size         APF Percent
  --------------- ----------------- -----------------------
        ----------------------- -----------------
         2 Kb   1638 Kb          0.00 Mb
                8.00 Mb          10
(return status = 0)
```

To change the size of the default data cache, enter:

```
sp_cacheconfig "default data cache", "30M"
```

This change is dynamic.

We know that to release or age out a data page from memory LRU strategy is applied. Even though the LRU replacement strategy is designed to keep popular or busy pages in memory, it is still possible that large queries and activities related to tempdb, may displace the popular data pages out of "Default data cache". This is indicated by High turnover in the sp_systemreports(discussed later). This can be resolved by configuring named caches.

A named cache is nothing but a user configured data cache. Each named cache , similar to "default data cache", contains a has table and single page buffers.

You can configure the named cache using the system procedure sp_cacheconfig.

For example,

```
sp_cacheconfig "test_cache", "15M"
```

This command creates a named cache called test_cache with size 15M.

You can drop the named cache using sp_cacheconfig.

Example:

```
sp_cacheconfig "test_cache", "0"
```

Consideration: Before dropping the named cache the objects or databases which are bound to the named cache must be "unbinded". Then the named cache is dropped. But the preallocated memory is released only after the adaptive server restart.

Binding a object/Database to named cache

Tempdb or a busy object is a candidate for binding into a named cache. As the object is dedicatedly bound to a named cache, this reduces the likely hood of the busy databases from being displaced from the cache. The object is now almost a memory resident and it reduces physical I/O.

The following example shows binding the sample database pubs2 to a named cache pubs2_cache.

```
>sp_bindcache 'pubs2_cache', 'pubs2'
>go
```

The following example shows binding a table "authors" of pubs2 database to the named cache pubs2_cache.

```
>sp_bindcache 'pubs2_cache', 'pubs2', 'authors'
>go
```

Unless the object/database is explicitly bound to a named cache, the referenced pages are read into the "Default Data cache" only.

To unbind the object/database from the named cache enter,

```
sp_unbindcache_all "cache_name"
```

You need to run the above command from the master database.

Other configuration parameters which affect memory

The parameters which affect the metadata structures and consume memory are,

- number of user connections
- number of locks
- open databases, open objects and indexes
- database devices

User Connections: The amount of memory needed per user connecton changes between platforms, and it is also dependent on other configuration parameters such as,

- default network packet size
- stack size

To change the user connections , enter:

```
sp_configure "number of user connections", new value
```

```
Parameter Name
         Default              Memory Used         Config Value
         Run Value            Unit
         Type
      ----------------------------------------------------------
--
      ---------------------- ---------------------- ------------
-----------
      ------------------------ ----------------------------------
------
      --------------------
number of user connections
                   25                   4153                  20
                   20                   number
         dynamic
```

```
(1 row affected)
Configuration option changed. ASE need not be rebooted since the
option is
dynamic.
Changing the value of 'number of user connections' to '20' reduces
the amount of
memory ASE uses by 18 K. The reduced memory may be reused when
this configure
value changes, but will not be released until ASE restarts.
(return status = 0)
```

The parameters that control the metadata caches in the server structure are number of open databases , number of open indexes, number of open objects, number of open partitions. To view the configured value and default values of these parameters use sp_configure system procedure.

Increase in the value of these parameters increases the memory of server structures.

The metadata caches for databases, indexes, partitions, objects will allow the adaptive server to gather metadata information from memory. This avoids expensive disk access and hence improves performance.

Number of locks: In a multiuser environment locks are basically used to access a data structure. When a process reads, or modifies a data structure it holds a lock on the data so that other user cannot simultaneously modify the data. Hence data integrity is protected.

Before a process acquires a shared, update or exclusive lock, the lock must be available in the shared memory. The number of locks are server wide setting and all the processes in adaptive server share a common pool of lock structures. The default value of number of locks is 5000, which is quite insufficient.

The required number of locks is estimated based on the expected number of concurrent user connections and the worker processes.It can be estimated as follows:

number of locks = (concurrent user connections + worker processes) x 20

Similarly the other parameters that uses memory are devices and disk I/O structures, paralell processing, remote servers using referential integrity constraints.

CHAPTER – 4
DEVICES AND DATABASES

DATABASE DEVICES

As we know that the server build utility will create three system devices namely

master
systemdbdev
sysprocsdev.

Then the databases master, model, tempdb and sybsystemdb , are built on master device. You can observe that the Tempdb database is also expanded into another device called tempdbdev device. Similarly sybsystemdb database is expanded into systemdbdev device.

You can view the databases and their mapping to the logical device using the system procedure

sp_helpdb <database_name>.

```
name                 db_size            owner              dbid
         created              durability        lobcomplvl
         inrowlen
         status
```

```
        ------------------------- ------------------------ ---
------- ----------

        ---------------------- --------------------- ----------
---------

        ---------------

        ------------------------------------------------------------
-------------------------------------------------------------------
-------------------------------------------------------
```

```
Master                          13.0 MB                     sa 1
         Feb 11,2014            full 0
             NULL
       mixed log and data
model                           3.0 MB                      sa 3
         Feb 11, 2014           full 0
              NULL
       mixed log and data
sybsystemdb                     6.0 MB                      sa 31513
         Feb 11, 2014           full 0
             NULL
       mixed log and data
sybsystemprocs                  172.0 MB                    sa 31514
         Feb 11, 2014           full 0
             NULL
      trunc log on chkpt, mixed log and data
tempdb                          104.0 MB                    sa 2
         Feb 11, 2014           no_recovery 0
             NULL
         select into/bulkcopy/pllsort, trunc log on chkpt, mixed
log and data, allow wide dol rows
(1 row affected)
```

Device

A database device is a storage space or resource which stores the objects that make up the databases. The term *device* refers to either a file in the file system or a disk partition.

Unlike other databases, the ASE uses the logical devices to manage the databases rather than the physical devices. This simplifies the administration. The logical device is nothing but a unique name that is mapped to either an operating system file or a disk partition. In the UNIX operating system the device is either a regular file or a raw partition. In WINDOWS operating system the device is created on NTFS file system.

Disk Initialization: Disk initialization is a process of preparing the RAW device or file system and making it known to the adaptive server before it can be used to store databases.

Creating and Dropping devices: The database devices are created by using disk init command. The disk init command basically does the following:

- The logical name of the device is mapped to the physical operating system file or to a RAW device.
- The new device entry is made into the sysdevices system table of the master database.
- It then prepares the device for database storage.

Device preparation: Basically the space within the device is uniformly divided into logical pages.

Figure (i) shows the depicts pages, extents and allocation units of a device.

The size of the logical pages can be 2K, 4K, 8K or 16K and this is configured while building the adaptive server itself, ie for a 2K server, the logical page size is 2K and the space within the device is uniformly divided in terms of 2K. Configuring the logical page is a server wide settingand this cannot be changed at all. All the devices you create should have the same logical page and it is not possible to create devices with different logical page size.

The logical page is a fundamental unit that the server either reads into the memory or writes from memory into the disk.

Extents

An extent is a group of eight pages. Eight contiguous logical pages are grouped to form an *Extent.*

Extents are logical and it is a fundamental unit for space allocation, i.e. whenever an object is created, a minimum of one extent is allocated to an object. As the table's data grows, further space is allocated in terms of extents. Similarly, when the data is shrunk, the space is deallocated in terms of extents.

Allocation Unit

A group of 32 extents is called as allocation unit. The disk init process basically divides the database device into allocation units, i.e, the device can be expressed in terms of allocation units.

A device is created with at least two allocation units. Each allocation unit contains 32 extents or 256 logical pages. Therefore for a 2K page server, the minimum size of the device is

2 allocation units x 256 pages x 2K = 1024Kbytes or 1MB

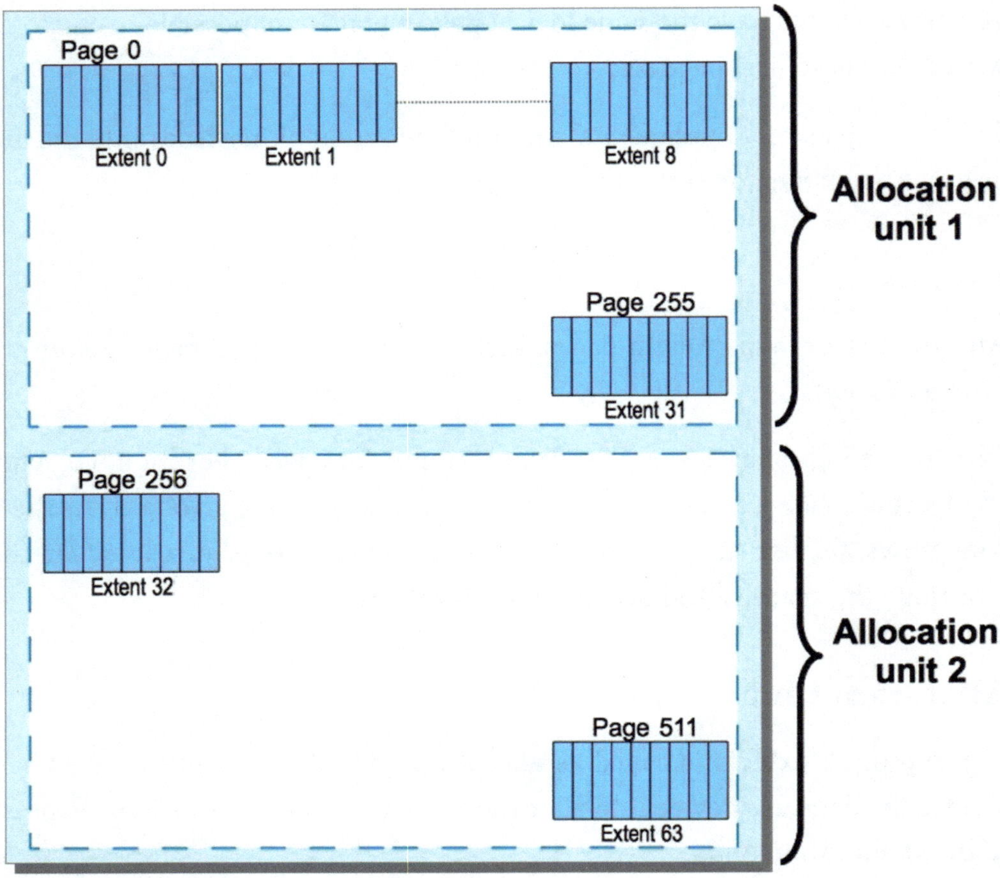

Fig. (i)

Disk init Syntax:

The database device is created using disk init command

```
disk init
name="logical_device_name",
physical name={"physical name"/"cache name"}
[vdevno=logical_device_number,]
size=number_of_blocks
[ , type='inmemory']
[ , vstart=logical_address,
cntrltype=controller_number]
[ , dsync={true/false}]
[ , instance="instance_name"]
```

NOTE: For the complete information and explanation of the Disk init command refer the Sybase Reference manual.

Few examples of creating a device:

```
    disk init
name='test_dev'
physname='/usr/sybase/DB_device/test_dev.dat',
size="10G"
```

test_dev is created with size 10 GB on the file system.

```
    disk init
name='test_dev1',
physname='/usr/sybase/DB_device/test_dev1.dat',
size=5120
```

test_dev1 device is created with size 10MB.The device size is specified in terms of number of logical pages.

```
    disk init
name='user_raw_device',
physname='/dev/rbc123',
vdevno=4,
size="50G"
```

user_raw_device device is created on a raw device with size 50GB.

```
    disk init
name='test_dev2',
physname='/usr/sybase/DB_device/test_dev2.dat',
skip_alloc "true"
size="10G"
```

With skip_alloc being "true" the Adaptive server does not allocate space during disk initialization.

Choice of a device - RAW versus Filesystem

Before ASE version 12.0, Sybase only supported raw partitions for device space allocation. Creating the device on the operating system file systems was not preferred. This was due to the fact that most file system had some kind of double buffering.

When the ASE writes to a device the data would actually be written to the operating system buffer and then written to the device. So the check point may not ensure writes to the device on the file system. This could be disastrous during instance crash, since whatever data stored in memory would be lost.

However with the changes in the file system which allow now direct writes to the device on a file, Sybase supports creating devices on file systems, provided the file system allows direct writes.

On the other hand RAW devices do not buffer their writes. Rather when the server issues a checkpoint, the data is directly written to the disk and writes are guaranteed. Apart from this, performance is also a consideration. In a write intensive environment, preferred choice would be to create devices on RAW partitions. In a read intensive environment devices on file system would perform better. As for as manageability is concerned, file systems are easier to manage than RAW partitions.

Dsync option: For the devices initialized on UNIX operating system files, the dsync option controls whether the writes to the files are buffered or not buffered. When dsync is on, it ensures that write to the device file occur directly and the ASE can recover the data on the device in the event of a system failure.

Directio option: The directio is a new parameter since ASE 15.0 version. When directio is set to "true", the adaptive server completely bypasses the operating system cache and transfers data directly to the disk. Directio performs I/O in the same manner as raw devices, and hence provides same performance benefits as raw devices. Since ASE version 15.5 you could create devices on file systems even for a write intensive environment.

The system procedure sp_helpdevice is used to get information about the devices and the mapping to the the file system or RAW devices.

```
Sp_helpdevice master
```

```
name                  db_size               owner               dbid
         created              durability         lobcomplvl
         inrowlen             status

      ------------ -------------------------- ---------- --------
      ------------------------ -------------------- -------------
-------
---------------- -------------------------------------

Master                13.0 MB              sa                   1
         Feb 11, 2014                  full 0
             NULL             mixed log and data

(1 row affected)
device_fragments

         size                 usage
         created
         free kbytes

      -----------------------------------------------------------
--

      --------------------------- -------------------------------
--------

      ---------------------------------------------------

      ---------------------------------

master

                      13.0 MB              data and log

             Feb 11 2014 5:17PM

                      4352

device                segment
------------ --------------------
master                default
master                logsegment
master                system
(return status = 0)
```

Dropping a device: To drop a device use system procedure sp_dropdevice:

```
sp_dropdevice logical name
```

When the device is dropped, the entry is removed from the sysdevices system table and vdevno is deallocated. This vdevno can be used to create other devices. However the file at the operating system will not be deleted. If the device has a database, it cannot be dropped. You must drop the database first and then the device.

Default devices: When the server is created, the master device is designated as a default device. When the database is created without explicitly specifying the device, the database is created on the master device. It is not advisable to create database on master device. You can make the user created device as a default device, and make master device as a non-default device.

To designate a user created device as default device, enter:

```
sp_diskdefault <new_device>, 'defaulton'
```

To make the master device as non-default device, enter:

```
sp_diskdefault master,'defaultoff'
```

The adaptive server can have multiple default devices.

Disk Resize: The database device can be expanded using disk resize command.

Example:

```
disk resize
name='test_dev',
size='5G'
```

The device test_dev is expanded by 5GB. The disk resize command adds space to the existing device. The database devices can only expand. They cannot be shrunk. When the device is expanded the **master..sysdevices** system table is updated. Creating a database device and disk resizing are executed by a user with sa_role.

Device Mirroring: The adaptive server provides you a method of protecting your database devices using disk mirroring. When a device is corrupted, you need to reinitialize devices which are mapped to disk drives and then restore the database through backups. This might have some downtime. You can avoid this with disk mirroring. Disk mirroring provides non-stop recovery in the event of media failure. Mirroring basically means that each write to a primary device is also written to a secondary device, so that you have duplicate copy of the data.

When a read or write to a mirrored device fails, the server unmirrors the damaged device and continues to write to the available device and records message in the error log.

By default, disk mirroring is disabled at the server level. In order to enable mirroring , the configuration option needs to be changed

```
sp_configure "disable disk mirroring", 0
```

It is a static parameter and it requires to reboot the adaptive server. To mirror a device called test_dev, issue the following command:

```
disk mirror
      name='test_dev'
      mirror='/usr/sybase/DB_device/test_dev_secondary.dat'
```

The disk mirror does not create another logical device. The primary and the mirrored device comprise one logical device. Once the device is mirrored, the server updates the master..sysdevices system table by changing the value of the status bit.

You can also specify the writes to be serial or noserial.

When the device is mirrored, the data in the primary device is copied into the secondary device. Then the subsequent data is written to both the devices.

Device Unmirroring: Any of the devices, either primary or secondary is automatically unmirrored when one of the device fails and the server records a message in the error log. You must remirror the device in order to restart mirroring.

Disk Unmirror Syntax:

```
disk unmirror
name="device_name",
[,side={'primary'/'secondary'}]
[,mode={retain/remove}]
```

When the device is unmirrored with mode=retain option, the unmirrored device can be remirrored. To permanently unmirror a device use mode=remove option.

To restart mirroring use the command:

```
disk remirror
name="device_name"
```

Restrictions on Resizing:

You cannot resize a device when it is mirrored. Use the disk resize command when the device is permanently unmirrored. The procedure for resizing a mirrored device is:

- Permanently unmirror the primary device.
- Increase the size of the primary device using disk resize command.
- Physically remove the mirror device if it is a regular file.
- Re-establish the mirroring process.

Relocating data to a new device:

If the database device is filled and there is no physical resource available for increasing the size of the device, then the database cannot be expanded off the same device. In this case you need to relocate the data to a new device. Sybase does not allow copying the data at the operating system level. Mirroring and unmirroring method can be used to relocate data.

Procedure:

1. Mirror the primary device to a file or a raw device of larger size

.

```
disk mirror
name='device_name',
mirror='mirror_file_name'
```

This process will copy the contents of a memory device to the new device

2. Then permanently unmirror the primary device.

```
Disk unmirror
name='device_name'
mode='remove'
side='primary'
```

Now you can resize the device as you have space available.

Mirroring Recommendations:

The main considerations for mirroring should be effects of system downtime, cost of storage and reduction in performance. Since the disk mirroring adds a write overhead, invariably the server performance will suffer.

- Mirror the master device to protect against downtime.
- As transaction logs are critical for possible recovery, mirror the devices on which the log segment is expanded.
- Do not mirror devices on which temporary databases are built.
- To mirror a database you need to mirror all the devices where the database segment is expanded.

DATABASES

A database is a logical container for all the data and objects needed for an application. Also the database is a basic unit of recovery. The database is created on a database device.

When the adaptive server is built, the installer process creates five system databases. All the system databases must be online and available for the functioning of the adaptive server.

Creating a Database:

Whenever a new database is created, the server uses a model database as a template and creates a new database. The purpose is to copy the system tables to the new database. Theses system tables store information about the database.

Database segments:

Every database when created contains by default three segments, namely:

Default
System
logsegment

A segment is a logical marker or a contiguous space allocated within a device or group of devices.

The default segment contains all the user objects.

The system segment has most of the system tables except syslogs table.

The logsegment has syslogs table. The default and system segment together is called a data segment.

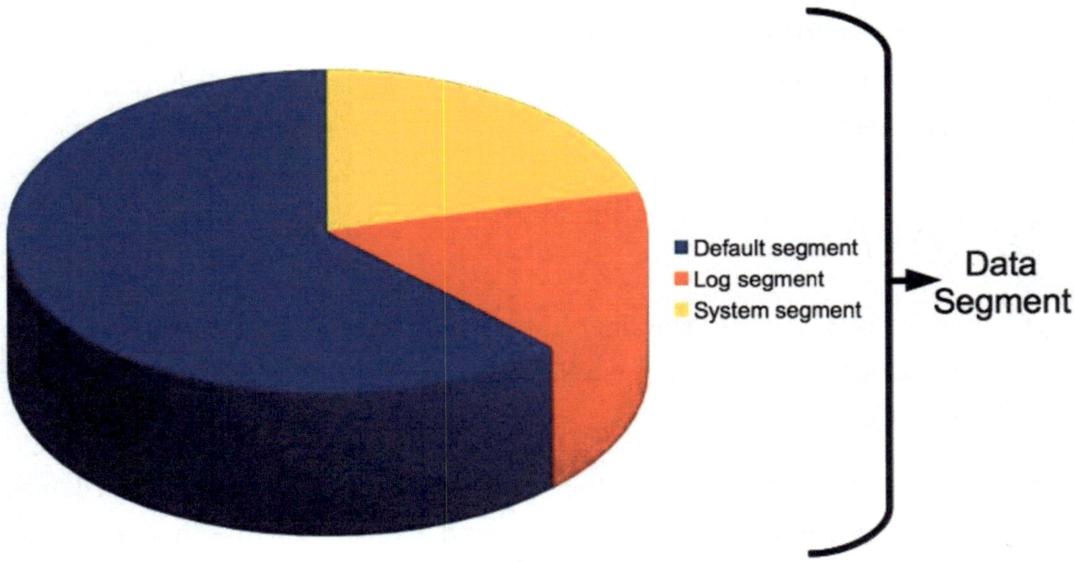

If we create a database on a single device the system segment, default segment and log segment are created on the same device. This is characterized by mixed log and data.

Apart from the system defined segments, the user can create a new segment.

Create database syntax:

```
create database database_name
```

```
on {default/database_device}[=size]
[log on database_device [=size]
with override
for load
```

Note: For the complete description of the create database command, refer the sybase Reference manual.

Following examples illustrates different ways of creating a database.

```
1. create database test_db
```

Creates a database test_db, on the default device and the size being equal to that of model.

```
2. Create database user_db
on device_name='100M'
```

user_db database is created on the specified device with size 100MB.

In the above two examples the database is created on a single device. Hence the system segment, default segment and logsegment are created on a single device. It is identified as "mixed log and data".

You could view the information about the new database using the system procedure sp_helpdb.

ex: **sp_helpdb**

```
name                 db_size              owner                dbid
        created              durability           lobcomplvl
        inrowlen
        status
        --------------------------- -------------------------- ---
------- ----------
        ------------------------ ---------------------- -----------
---------
        ----------------
        -----------------------------------------------------------
-------------------------------------------------------------

db                   3.0 MB               sa                   5
```

```
          Feb 18, 2014                  full              0
              NULL
          Mixed               log       and       data

master             13.0 MB              sa                1

          Feb 11, 2014                  full              0
              NULL
       mixed log and data

model              3.0 MB               sa                3

          Feb 11, 2014                  full 0
             NULL
        mixed log and data

sybsystemdb        6.0 MB               sa                31513

          Feb 11, 2014                  full              0
              NULL
        mixed log and data

sybsystemprocs              172.0 MB             sa       31514

          Feb 11, 2014                  full 0
              NULL
    trunc log on chkpt, mixed log and data

tempdb             104.0 MB             sa                2

          Feb 11, 2014                  no_recovery       0
              NULL
      select into/bulkcopy/pllsort, trunc log on chkpt, mixed log
and data, allow wide dol rows

testdb             3.0 MB               sa                4

          Feb 12, 2014                  full              0
              NULL
        mixed log and data

(1 row affected)
```

Consideration: If the database is created on a single device with mixed log and data, the server does not allow taking backup of transaction logsegment. You need to take full database backup. In the case of failure of the device, you lose both data and logsegment. You can restore database from the full database backup. So the point of recovery falls back to the date of your most recent database backup. You cannot perform point in time or up to the minute recovery.

It is always recommended to create the database by separating the data segment from the logsegment and on separate devices.

```
Create database salesdb

      on data_dev='10M'
      log on log_dev='5M'
      go
```

salesdb is created with data segment on data_dev and size 10MB.

Log segment is created on log_dev with size 5MB. The total size of the database is 15MB.

```
create database practisedb

      on data_dev1='10M', data_dev2='15M'
      log on
      log_dev1='5M', log_dev2='5M'
      go
```

The practicedb database is created, with datasegment on two devices namely data_dev1 and data_dev2. Logsegment is created on two devices namely log_dev1 and log_dev2. The total size of the database is 35MB.

For load option:

If you are creating a database to load a database dump , you can use "for load" option. When you create a new database the server clears all the pages in the database device. This process takes more time.

If you are using for load option for creating the database, it skips the page clearing step and creates the database.

The database is created in a streamlined process and it is approximately 250 times faster than normal database creation. This saves time.

However the database created with for load option is not accessible. The only commands that will work on such a database are alter database for load, load database, drop database.

Once you load the database from the database dump, there will be no restrictions on the commands.

With override option:

Creating the database with override options allows you to separate the data segment and log segment, but still it allows to create the two separated segments on the same device. Sybase does not recommend creating a database with override option.

However, if you have very limited storage space on your machine, creating databases with override may be your only option.

As the log segment and data segment is separated within a single device, you can dump your transaction log. Risk factor is that in case of media failure, you cannot access the current log and upto the minute recovery is not possible.

```
create database sampledb

      on sample_dev='10M'
      log on sample_dev='4M'
      with override
```

System Tables Affected by Create database

When a database is created a row is added to master..sysdatabases system table. As the database is built on a device or devices, the space allocation information is recorded in the table master..sysusages.

The space allocated for the database in a device is called a database fragment. For example, if the database is built on three devices, then there will be three database or device fragments. So three rows are entered in the master..sysusages system table indicating the size and logical starting disk address for that fragment.

The database is uniquely identified by a name and DBID. This information along with other attributes of the database is stored in sysdatabases table.

Database owner:

When a new database is created, by default a user is created within the database called *database owner.* The database owner has all the object level permissions to manage his own schema and object own by other users as well.

When the database is created by 'sa', sa will become the owner of the database. In general, the creator of the database will be the owner of the database.

Even though the database can be created by any login who has sa_role or create database permission, in majority of the environments the database is created by the system administrator('sa' login) in order to centralize the control of database placement. It is a practice that the 'sa' creates databases on behalf of the other users and then transfers the ownership to other logins.

The database name, ownership, DBID, database options can be viewed by using the system stored procedure sp_helpdb.

To change the ownership to other logins enter:

```
sp_changedbowner login_name
```

Restrictions: This procedure is to be executed from the current database whose ownership needs to be changed.

The login should not be already user of the database. The change in ownership information is updated in sysdatabases system table.;

Database options:

Just like the configuration parameters control the behavior of adaptive server, we have Database options at the database level. Database options can be viewed as parameters which control the behavior of a database.

They control-

- Table column defaults
- Database recovery and bcp operations
- Log behavior
- Restriction to user access

The system administrators or database owners can change the database options.

To view the database options use the system procedure sp_dboptions without any argument.

```
sp_dboption
```

```
Settable database options.
database_options
----------------------------------------------------------------
abort tran on log full
allow nulls by default
allow wide dol rows
async log service
auto identity
dbo use only
ddl in tran
delayed commit
enforce dump tran sequence
full logging for all
full logging for alter table
full logging for reorg rebuild
full logging for select into
identity in nonunique index
no chkpt on recovery
no free space acctg
read only
scratch database
select into/bulkcopy/pllsort
single user
trunc log on chkpt
trunc. log on chkpt.
unique auto_identity index
(23 rows affected)
(return status = 0)
```

Single User – The database will allow only one user to access the database at a time. Typically is used when performing maintenance tasks. Tempdb database cannot be run in single user mode.

Dbo use only – The database can be accessed only by dbo.

Read only – The database is read only and no modifications can be done.

Allow nulls by default – Any new table created in the database allows null values in a column by default.

Auto identity – It forces all the tables to be built with a column called SYB_IDENTITY_COL, even though the table does not have identity property a primary key or a unique key constraint.

Identity in non unique index – This option makes the existing identity column to use a non-unique index. The additional unique column will allow the index to be effectively unique.

Unique auto-identity index – Automatically creates an IDENTITY column with a unique, non-clustered index for new tables.

Select into/blk copy/pll sort – Performs minimally logged operations on the specified database for select into, bcp operations and parallel sort.

full logging for all

```
full logging for alter table
full logging for reorg rebuild
full logging for select into
```

As of ASE version 15.7 a few alter table operations such as alter table adding a non-null column, data movement from source table to destination table using "select into", "reorg and rebuilding" of objects- all these operations can be now performed in a full logged mode. These operations do not invalidate the transaction log dumps and hence do not break the log dump sequence.

When "full logging for all" is set to true, no need to individually set full logging for select into, full logging for alter table, full logging for reorg build.

NOTE: Full logging for fast bcp and parallel sort is not yet supported and cannot be done unless you set select into/bulk copy/pll sort to true.

"select into/bulk copy/pll sort" dboption and "full logging" are mutually exclusive i.e both the options cannot be true.

Enforce dump tran sequence – When this option is set to true, it disallows any operations which forces minimally logged operations in a database which prevents from taking a dump transaction. This option can be set in a database where the log segment is on its own device.

Abort tran on log full – When the logsegment last chance threshold is crossed, the running transactions are aborted.

Truncate log on chkpt – The transaction logsegment is automatically truncated and space is cleaned when the server issues a free checkpoint.

No free space acctg – This option suppresses free space accounting and execution of threshold actions for the non log segments. This speeds up the recovery time.

No checkpoint on recovery – This option is set on a secondary database in a DR setup. During the recovery process checkpoint is not issued on the secondary database. Hence the transaction log dumps from the primary database can be sequentially added into the secondary database.

Using sp_dboption to change he database option

The database options can be changed using system procedure sp_dboption. You need to be in master database to execute sp_dboption.

Here is an example-

```
>use master
>go
>sp_dboption salesdb, 'single user', 'true'
>go
```

The database option for salesdb is changed and now only one user can access salesdb database at a time.

When the database option is changed, the sysdatabases system table in master is updated. This is reflected in the status column of sysdatabases.

Once the database option is changed, the server automatically issues a checkpoint.

To revert back to the default option issue:

```
>use master
```

```
>go
>sp_dboption salesdb 'single user', 'false'
>go
```

The database salesdb is brought back to multiuser mode.

Sizing the Database

The user database should be large enough to hold the application data that is entered into it. While estimating the size of the database we need to consider the size of the tables, indexes and anticipated growth of the data. Note that the database can only expand and they cannot be shrunk. So it is always better to under estimate the size of the database rather than unnecessarily over estimating the size and creating a large database. This will impact the backup and restoration time and may exceed your business defined recovery window.

The adaptive server includes a system procedure called sp_estspace, through which you can compute the estimated size of the table based on the number of rows you add.

Example:

```
>sp_estspace "accounts", 20000
>go
```

It provides information about the space needed to add 20000 records for accounts table. The system procedure sp_estspace also computes the size of the indexes if they exists, for the table.

Alter database command is used to expand the database.

Example:

```
>alter database salesdb
     >on sales_data_dev1='50M'
     >log on sales_log_dev1='10M'
```

The database salesdb is expanded and a space of 50MB is allocated on sales_data_dev1 for the data segment. A space of 10MB is allocated for the log segment on the device sales_log_dev1.

The space allocation and device fragment information is stored on the sysusages system table found in the master database.

NOTE: As of ASE version 15.7 the logsegment can be shrunk.

Dropping the Database

To drop a database which is no longer required , issue:

```
>drop database database_name
```

The command must be issued from master database.

Restrictions:

- The database currently in use cannot be dropped.
- You cannot drop the database referenced by other database.
- The database owner or a login with sa_role can drop a database.
- A corrupt database which is in the suspect mode cannot be dropped.

Multiple Temporary Databases and Management

The installer process creates a system temporary database called tempdb along with other system databases.

To view the information about tempdb enter:

```
>sp_helpdb tempdb
```

For a 2K page server, the size of the tempdb is 104MB. 4MB space is allocated in the master device and 100MB space is allocated in tempdbdev device. The tempdb is a temporary workspace which is available to the users as well as to the server.

When a session is established, the user is allocated with a workspace in the temporary database. If the tempdb is full and if the server is unable to allocate a workspace , the new login session fails and the existing sessions cannot perform most of the queries. So sizing and managing the tempdb is a very important aspect for the adaptive server.

The uses of tempdb are:

- Any user can create object in tempdb called session specific temporary tables.
- The adaptive server also uses tempdb for calculating aggregates, sorting data and to store intermediate results from union and join statements.

Tempdb size:

The size of the tempdb should be greater than the size of the model database. Because the tempdb database is not recovered during server restarts, tempdb is recreated by the server every time the adaptive server is restarted. When the model database is expanded we need to expand the tempdb as well.

Consideration: If tempdb is very small, the queries which triggers sort operation and which may require space in tempdb will fail. So resize the tempdb based on the total number of user connections, based on the space required when running the largest query.

Issues with tempdb:

Having a single tempdb for the server may lead to performance issues as listed below.

- In a multiuser environment, if more users tend to access tempdb, it leads to contention on memory and disk resources because multiple users compete for space within single tempdb.
- Creating and dropping more session specific tables in a single tempdb lead to contention on system tables within the tempdb.
- A runaway process may always fill a space in tempdb. This affects all other users.

As a solution, Sybase ASE allows creating multiple temporary databases.

- Reduces contention on system tables as users are distributed across the multiple temporary databases.

- Workload can be uniformly shared across multiple temporary databases.
- Automatic load balancing can be achieved.
- You can exclusively dedicate a temporary database for 'sa' login or to a heavy user.

Creating Multiple temporary databases

User created temporary databases have characteristics similar to the system temp_db. They are-

- Used to create temporary objects.
- All the temporary databases are recreated during system recovery. Hence all the user created objects are lost during shutdown or system crash.
- When the temporary databases are created, they use model database as a template. But in addition to that,
- Status column in sysdatabases is updated, indicating temporary nature of the database.
- Database option "selectinto/bulkcopy/pllsort" is set to true. This allows creation of copy tables.
- Database option "trunc log on chkpt" is enabled. Hence, log management is not necessary and there is no need to create data and log segment on separate devices.
- "guest" user is created so that all the users do not need exclusive permission to access temporary database.
- "create table" permission is granted to public.

Example for creating temporary database:

```
>create temporary database tempdb01
>on tempdb01_data_dev=500
>log on tempdb01_log_dev=100
```

Dropping temporary database

Just like a normal database, the temporary database can be dropped.

```
>drop database database_name
```

Restrictions: If any sessions are active, the database cannot be dropped.

If the login is bounded to the temporary database, unbind the login before dropping the database.

If the temporary database is part of a default group, it cannot be dropped. Remove from the group before dropping the database.

Creating a temporary database group

A group is a logical set of one or more temporary databases. The system database "tempdb" is a default member of group. The name of the group is "default".

In order to view the group information and the login binding information use the system procedure sp_tempdb.

Example:

```
>sp_tempdb 'show'
```

```
Temporary Database Groups

-------------------------------------------------------

default

(1 row affected)

Database                    GroupName
-------------------- ----------------------
tempdb                      default

(1 row affected)

Login                       Application                 Group
         Database           Hardness

      -------------- -------------------------- -----------------
---------------
      -------------------- -------------------------------------

(0 rows affected)
(return status = 0)
```

As you could see, the group by name "default" has only one member, namely tempdb.

Characteristics of a group assignment

- The server always has a temporary database group by name "default". The default group can neither be dropped nor renamed.
- When new temporary databases are created, they are created as standalone databases. You need to add the temporary databases explicitly to the default group.

Example: To add the temporary database tempdb01 to the default group issue.

```
>sp_tempdb 'add', tempdb01, 'default'
>go
```

Similarly to remove tempdb01 from the default group issue:

```
>sp_tempdb 'remove', tempdb01, 'default'
>go
```

You need to bind the logins exclusively either to the "default" group or to the standalone temporary database. If the logins are not bound to the group or stand alone temporary database, they will be always assigned to the system tempdb.

Example: To bind the login to the default group, enter:

```
>sp_tempdb 'bind', lg, login_name, gr, 'default'
>go
```

Example: To bind a login exclusively to the temporary database, enter:

```
>sp_tempdb 'bind', lg, login_name, db, tempdb01
>go
```

When the login is part of a default group, the login is assigned to any one of the available temporary database within the default group. The member of the default group for assigning to a login is chosen based on a round robin policy.

Example: To view the temporary database assigned to the login, enter:

```
>select db_name(@@ tempdbid)
```

```
>go
```

- The active session which has been assigned a temporary database will continue to use the database even though the bindings have changed. Any changes in the binding will be effective from the next session.

To unbind a login, enter:

```
>sp_tempdb 'unbind', lg, login _name
```

Isolating 'sa' login

It is recommended to isolate 'sa' login from other logins of the server. A situation may arise where heavy activities of other applications and logins may fill the tempdb. This will block the 'sa' login to connect to the server. You can avoid this by exclusively binding 'sa' login to a dedicated temporary database.

Example:

```
>sp_tempdb bind, lg, sa, db, tempdb_sa
```

To view the active login assigned to a temporary database, enter:

```
>sp_tempdb 'who', 'tempdb01'
>go
```

CHAPTER – 5
USER MANAGEMENT

OVERVIEW

After installing the adaptive server, one of the major tasks of the system administrator is to set up a secure administrative environment. This task includes-

- Assigning login names to system administrators and system security officers and to establish password and login policies.
- Granting roles to individual users and enable auditing to ensure individual accountability.
- Create database users and groups. Administer the permissions for users, groups and roles.
- These aspects are discussed in this chapter.

ACCESSING DATA

The adaptive server has a three layered approach to allow the end user to access data.

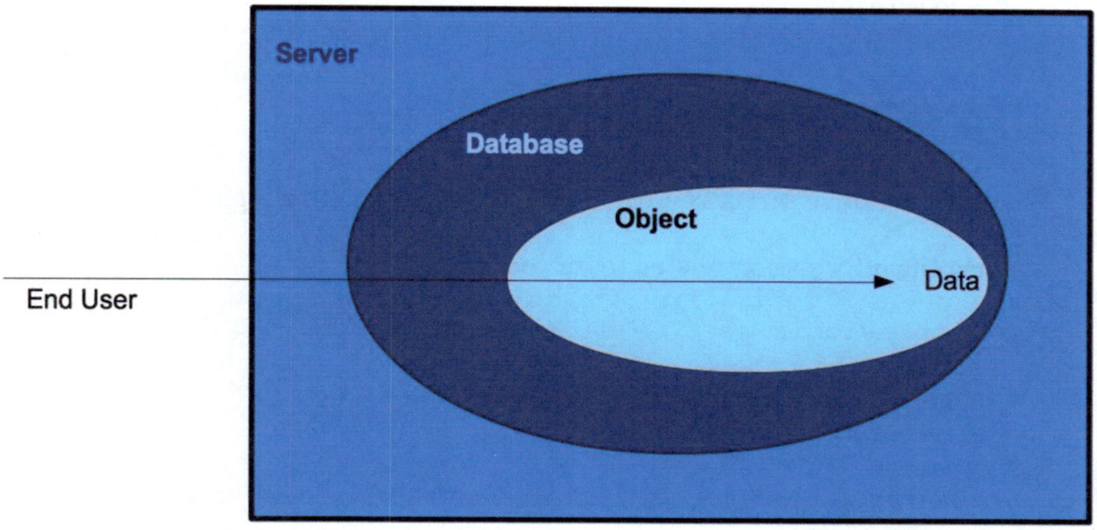

In order to access data:

- The end user must login to the server. This is done by using a valid login name and password.

For example, we connect to the server using isql utility:

```
isql -Usa -P<password> -S<server_name>
```

By default the end user will connect to the master database.

To verify the database you have established connection enter:

```
>select db_name()
>go
```

- Then the end user needs to connect to the database before accessing the data. In order to use the database, the end user or login must have a mapping to the user of the database, i.e, the login must be a valid user of the database.

For example, to use database "salesdb" enter:

```
>use salesdb
>go
```

- Finally, in order to access the data, the end user must have object level permissions.

THE 'SA' LOGIN

When the adaptive server is created, it is configured with a login 'sa'.

To view the information related to 'sa' login, enter:

```
>sp_displaylogin sa

Suid: 1
Loginame: sa
Fullname:
Default Database: master
Default Language:
Auto Login Script:
Configured Authorization:
      sa_role (default ON)
      sso_role (default ON)
      oper_role (default ON)
      sybase_ts_role (default ON)
Locked: NO
Date of Last Password Change: Feb 11 2014 5:17PM
Password expiration interval: 0
Password expired: NO
Minimum password length: 6
Maximum failed logins: 0
Current failed login attempts:
Authenticate with: AUTH_DEFAULT
Login Password Encryption: SHA-256
Last login date: Feb 19 2014 12:54PM
Exempt inactive lock: 0
(return status = 0)
```

By default the 'sa' login is associated with system roles.

```
sa_role
sso_role
oper_role
sybase_ts_role
```

i.e, the login is configured with both system administration role and system security officer role. Hence 'sa' login has unlimited power. The 'sa' login is configured with NULL password. Change the 'sa' login password immediately after server installation.

```
>sp_password NULL, <new_password>, sa
>go
```

It is recommended not to allow multiple users to use 'sa' login. Rather, create individual logins and enforce accountability by assigning individual roles.

Creating a new login

Logins are server wide and a new login is created using the system procedure sp_addlogin.

When a new login is created the server assigns a unique id called "suid" and a record is added to syslogins system table in the master database.

A few examples of creating logins is listed as follows:

```
>sp_addlogin "surya", "10@comp456"
```

The above example creates a login surya with the password 10@comp456. The login uses master database as default database.

```
>sp_addlogin abdul, omar321, salesdb
```

A login by name abdul is created with default database salesdb.

NOTE: For a full list of options associated with sp_addlogin, refer sybase reference manual documentation.

When a login is created, it can be associated with the following attributes-

default database(defdb) – It is the default database. Login will be connected to the specified default database at the start of each session.

default language(deflanguage) – The language in which the user's prompts and messages are displayed. By default the language chose is English.

full name – Full name of the user. It is helpful for documentation purpose.

password expiration(passwdexp) – By default the passwords do not expire and the default value is zero. The value must be specified in the number of days.

The following example shows adding a login with default database, default language, full name and password expiration.

```
>sp_addlogin mark, "200mark@x23", salesdb, french, "mark twain", 40
```

minimum password length(minpwdlen) – The default password length is 6. It can be changed server wide by using sp_configure or explicitly by specifying with sp_addlogin.

Example:

```
>sp_configure minimum password length, 5
>go
```

Example:

```
>sp_addlogin grace, grace123 @minpwdlen=8
```

Dropping a login-

To drop a login use system procedure sp_droplogin login_name

Restrictions: 'sa' login cannot be dropped. A login who has a user in a database and owns objects cannot be dropped.

Login modification-

The attributes of a login can be modified using sp_modifylogin system procedure.

For example:

```
>sp_modifylogin abdul, defdb, testdb
```

The default database is changed to testdb.

Locking a login-

In order to deny access to objects owned by an active database user lock the login account.

Example:

```
>sp_locklogin login name, 'lock'
```

To unlock a login, issue:

```
>sp_locklogin login_name, 'unlock'
```

Database user

A database user is nothing but a mapping for a login to access a database, i.e, in order to access a database, a login must be listed as a user of the database.

When a new database is created, the creator of the database(usually sa) is mapped to a database user **dbo**. The user '**dbo**' is called as 'database owner' which means to say that all the databases are created with a default user called **dbo**, who is mapped to the creator of the database(usually sa). This is depicted as follows:

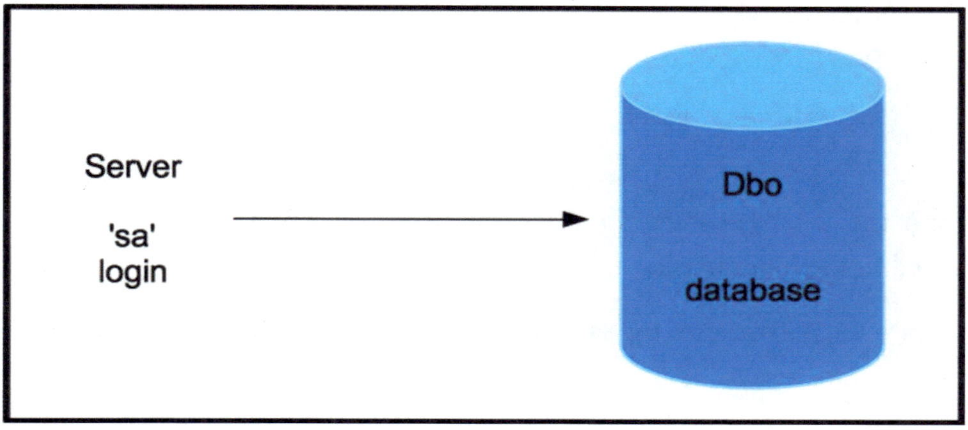

When 'sa' login or any login with 'sa_role' accesses a database, he will be using the database as a '**dbo**'.

Role of a dbo

A database owner can perform the following activities within the database.

- Creating and dropping users of the database and to grant and revoke permissions to create database objects.
- A 'dbo' can backup and load databases and transactions logs.
- Execute checkpoint and run database consistency(dbcc) commands.
- Set database options

Creating a Database user

When a database user is created the adaptive server verifies the existence of a login in the syslogins system table present in the master database and then the new user is listed in the sysusers system table. The database user is uniquely assigned with a user id called "uid".

Example:

```
>sp_adduser login_name, [,user_name] [,group_name]
```

To create a database user is as same as the login name issue:

```
>sp_adduser login_name
```

Example:

```
>use salesdb
>go

>sp_adduser mark
>go
```

Within the database sales db a database user by name 'mark' is created who is mapped to the login mask.

To create a database user by name mark_test for the login mark in the database test issue:

```
>use test
>go

>sp_adduser mark, mark_test
>go
```

The database user mark_test is created in the database 'test'. The user is mapped to the login 'mark'.

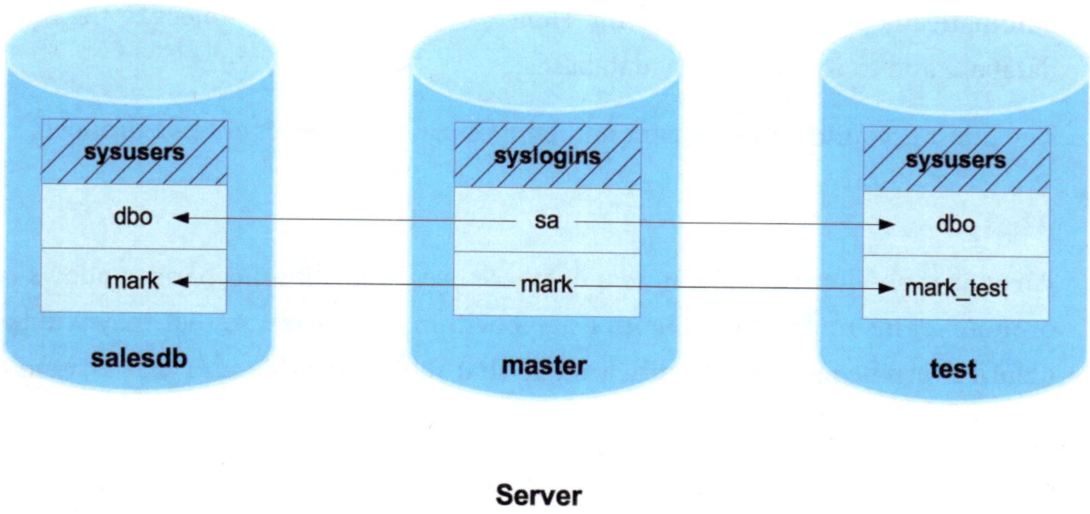

Characteristics of User and login mapping

- A single login can have a user in multiple databases. Hence a login can access multiple databases
- A single cannot have multiple users within a database. Therefore a login cannot become a database owner if the login already has a database user.
- A database user cannot use multiple login name (with the exception of alias)

To view the information about users, issue:

```
>sp_helpuser
>go
```

Guest user:

The "guest" is a special kind of database user, which is mapped to any login.

Example: To create a guest user in any database issue:

```
>sp_adduser guest
```

If a database has a guest user, any login can access that database, without having a valid user within the database.

When the adaptive server is created, a guest user is automatically created in the master database and tempdb. The user created temporary databases will also automatically have a guest account. Hence, every login can connect to the master database and to the temporary databases.

The guest accounts in the master and temporary databases cannot be dropped.

Aliases

An alias is an alternative login to a database user. The alias mechanism allows two or more logins to use the same user name within a database, so that they will have identical privileges. It is often helpful so that more than one user can assume the role of database owner.

Also you can utilize the alias mechanism to set up a collective user identity.

Adding a alias

To add an alias, use the system procedure:

```
>sp_addalias login_name, user_name
```

Example:

The login mark has a database user mark_test in the test database. The login 'abdul' do not have a user in the database test. In order for the login 'abdul' to access the test database we can add an alias.

```
>sp_addalias abdul, mark_test
```

Information on the alias is stored in the 'sysalternates' system table.

To drop an alias, issue:

```
>sp_dropalias login_name
```

User Impersonation

The purpose of using a server is to acquire permissions of another user and his identity.

Only a database owner can use the server command to impersonate another users identity.

This allows the database owner to-

- access an object owned by another user
- a dbo can create objects that will be owned by another user
- grant permissions on an object owned by another user
- Syntax:

```
>setuser [user_name]
```

For example:

```
>setuser "williams"
```

To verify the login and database user, issue:

```
>select suser_name( ), user_name( )
>go
```

The impersonation ends when-

- another setuser command is executed
- current database is changed

PERMISSIONS

As discussed in the beginning of the chapter, in order to access data from a table, view or to execute a procedure, the end user should have permission on the object.

Who can grant a permission?

- The object owners can grant permissions to access their objects to other database users.
- The object owners can also grant other users the ability to pass the access permissions to other database users.
- The permissions are grantable to database users, groups within the database and to roles.
- The permissions are granted with "grant" command and the permissions can be withdrawn using "revoke" command.
- The grant and revoke commands can give permissions to:

- create a database
- execute dbcc
- create objects within a database
- access tables, views and specified columns of a table

The following figure depicts the hierarchy of permissions.

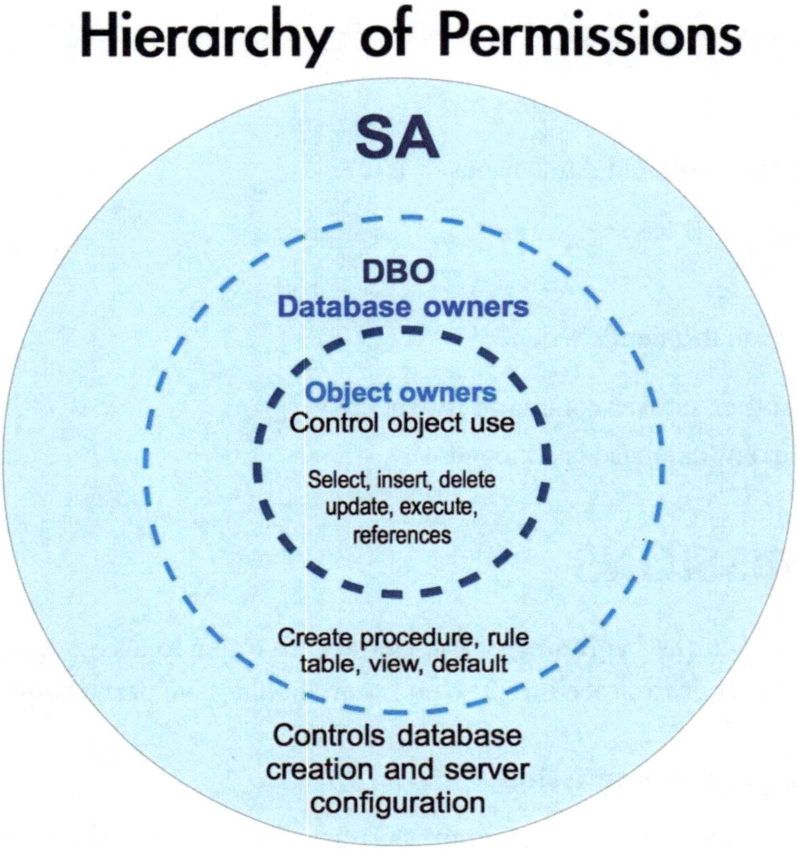

Restrictions on permissions

Ownership of objects cannot be transferred, i.e, schema remapping is not allowed.

Database owners do not automatically get permissions on objects owned by other users.

A database owner can only temporarily acquire the permissions of a user by using setuser command. Permissions are not required to use a “default”, “rules”, “user defined databases","cursors". Permissions are not required to create indexes and triggers on a table.

Examples:

- To grant read/modify permission on a table named accounts to all the users issue:

```
>grant all
>on accounts to public
```

To grant select permission on only a few selected columns of authors table to the database user mark_test, issue:

```
>grant select on authors(au_lname, au_fname) to mark_test
```

With grant option

With grant option within a grant statement permits the user to further grant permissions to other users. This option must be sparingly used.

Example:

>Grant insert on titles

>to mark

>with grant option

Result:

- mark can insert into titles
- mark can grant insert permission on the table titles to other users

```
>grant insert on titles
>to ruby
```

- >revoke insert on titles from mark

Result: mark cannot insert into table titles. Mark cannot further grant permission to other database users. Any user who has already received insert into permission from mark will lose the permissions.

Use the system procedure sp_helprotect to view all the permissions assigned.

Example:

```
>sp_helprotect titles
```

Lists all the types of permissions on table titles which is assigned to all the users.

```
>sp_helprotect mark
```

Lists all the permissions that mark has in the database.

```
>sp_helprotect it_role
```

Lists the permissions granted to the role it_role.

```
>sp_helprotect mark, null, null, "granted"
```

Lists the information on all the roles granted to the user mark.

```
>sp_helprotect mark, null, null, "enabled"
```

List the information on all the active roles granted to mark.

The permission information related to the objects is stored in the system table called sysprotects.

Section - 4
Groups

A group is a collection of database users.

Groups provide a convenient method to grant and revoke permissions to many users in a single statement.

Groups are database specific and they are not server wide meaning that the groups exists within the database.

To view the information about groups, issue:

```
>sp_helpuser
>go
```

sp_helpuser displays the database users and their respective groups.
As you could see, every database has a group by name "public".
The group "public" cannot be dropped from a database.
Every user is automatically a member of a group.
In order to grant a permission to all users simply grant the permission to "public".

Creating and changing groups

A database owner can create a group using:

```
>sp_addgroup "group_name"
```

Example:

```
>use salesdb
>go
>sp_addgroup IT_team
>go
```

A group by name IT_team is created in the database salesdb.

A user can be added to the group using:

```
>sp_changegroup group_name, user_name
```

Example:

```
>sp_changegroup IT_group, mark
```

The database user mark will be changed from public group to IT_group.

Alternatively, the user can be added to a group while creating the user in the database.

Example:

```
>sp_adduser subhodh, subhodh_salesdb, IT_team
```

A database user subhodh_salesdb is created and he is member of IT_team group.

To drop a user from a DBO defined group and reassign to public group issue:

```
>sp_changegroup "public", mark
```

Now mark is a member of public group.

To drop a group from the database use:

```
>sp_dropgroup IT_team
>go
```

Restriction:

- Within the database domain a user can be part of a single group. A database user cannot be part of a multiple group.
- Group is database wide, not server wide. So a group cannot contain multiple users from different databases.
- Groups are not hierarchal, i.e, a group cannot contain other groups
- As all the users are members of a public group, any kind of permission assigned to a "public" group is automatically assigned to all the users. In order too exclude or remove permissions from a few users, you need to execute explicit revoke statements individually.
- A role cannot be assigned to a group.

ROLES

A role is a collection of permissions. The roles are being supported be adaptive server in order to enforce individual accountability.

A role can be either a system defined role or user defined role.

System defined roles

The following table lists the system defined roles and their description.

ROLE	ROLE NAME	DESCRIPTION

System Administrator	sa_role	Maintain ASE databases and disk storage
System Security Officer (SSO)	sso_role	Allowed to perform security related tasks
Operator	oper_role	Perform dump and load of the database server wide
Sybase technical support	sybase_ts_role	Execute certain dbcc commands for database analysis
Attributed transaction manager	dtm_tm_role	Transaction coordination across remote servers
Replication	replication_role	Replicate user data
Monitor and diagnosis	mon_role	Needed to access MDA tables
High availability	ha_role	Execute fail over in a clustered environment
Job scheduler user	JS_user_role	Create and run jobs using Job Scheduler
Real time messaging	messaging_role	Execute real time messaging
Web services	web_services	Web services Administration

System roles associated with 'sa' login

In order to display the roles associated with sa login, use:

```
>sp_displaylogin 'sa'
>go
```

```
Suid: 1
Loginame: sa
Fullname:
Default Database: master
Default Language:
Auto Login Script:
```

```
Configured Authorization:
sa_role (default ON)
sso_role (default ON)
oper_role (default ON)
sybase_ts_role (default ON)
Locked: NO
Date of Last Password Change: Feb 11 2014 5:17PM
Password expiration interval: 0
Password expired: NO
Minimum password length: 6
Maximum failed logins: 0
Current failed login attempts:
Authenticate with: AUTH_DEFAULT
Login Password Encryption: SHA-256
Last login date: Feb 19 2014 12:54PM
Exempt inactive lock: 0
(return status = 0)
```

The roles associated with 'sa' login are:

sa_role
sso_role
oper_role
sybase_ts_role

You could see that by default all these roles are enabled.

System Administrator Privileges

A login with sa_role can perform the following activities.

- Modify the configuration parameters related to security
- Create, modify server logins and assign passwords
- Set the attributes of a login such as changing minimum length of the password, set password expiration interval, etc.
- Create and manage user defined roles.
- Grant and revoke SSO and open roles to other logins.
- Audit system management.
- Lock, unlock and drop logins

The system roles are enabled by default. You can temporarily disable the system roles.

Example:

```
>set role sa_role off
```

The disable role can be reenabled using:

```
>set role sa_role on
```

or by logging out and starting a new session.

Recovering passwords for SSO logins

Only a login with SSO_role has the authorization to change the passwords of other users. In the eventuality of losing the password, you can regenerate the password for sa login or for any login with SSO_role.

Procedure:

- Shut down the adaptive server.
- Edit the RUNSERVER script and add the -p option to the data server command.

```
#!/bin/sh
#
# ASE page size (KB): 2048
# Master device path: /sybase/data/Test_master.dat
# Error log path: /sybase/ASE-15_0/install/Test.log
# Configuration file path: /sybase/ASE-15_0/Test.cfg
# Directory for shared memory files: /sybase/ASE-15_0
# Adaptive Server name: Test
#
/sybase/ASE-15_0/bin/dataserver \
-d/sybase/data/Test_master.dat \
-e/sybase/ASE-15_0/install/Test.log \
-c/sybase/ASE-15_0/Test.cfg \
-M/sybase/ASE-15_0 \
-sTest \
```

-p

~

- Restart the server
- The -p option makes the adaptive server to regenerate the password and display the password at the console.
- Login to the server using the regenerated password.
- Set a new password.

Example:

```
>sp_password 'regenerated_password', <new_password>, sa
```

System Tables associated to Roles

When a new role is created, the new role is assigned a unique id called 'srid' and the information is stored in syssrvroles system table found in the master database.

When the role is assigned to a login, the server checks for the suid and login name in the syslogins system table.

Then the 'suid' and 'srid' information is added to the system table sysloginroles found in the master database.

The following diagram depicts the relation between syslogins, syssrvroles, sysloginroles and sysusers system tables.

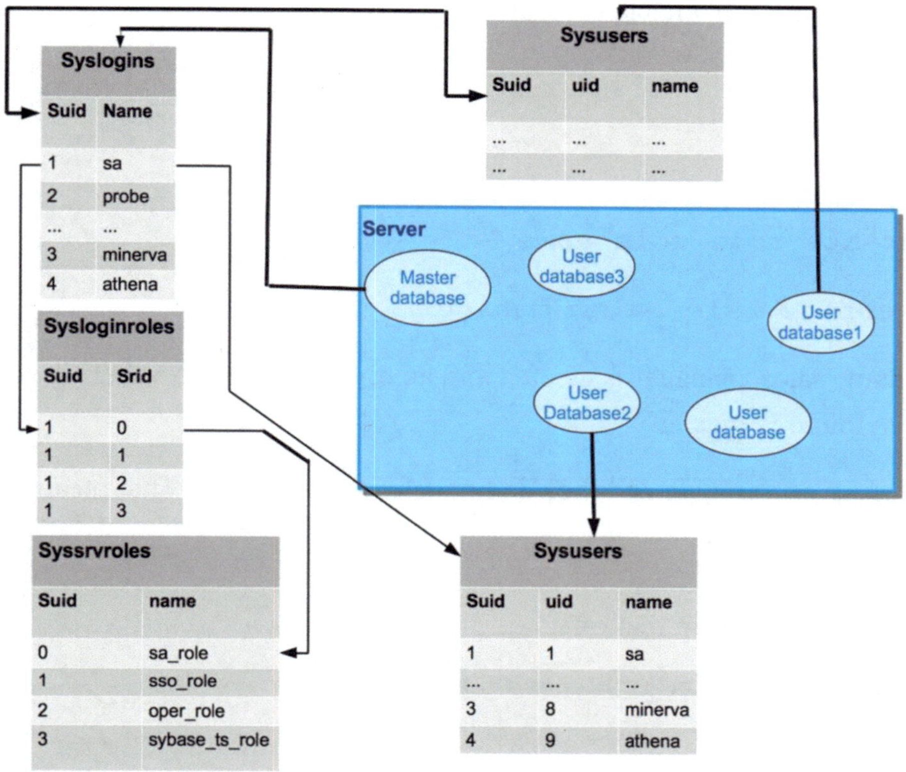

User Defined roles

A user defined role is a collection of permissions.

Characteristics of a role:

The roles are server wide

- A single login can use multiple roles.
- The roles are hierarchal, meaning that a role can be assigned to another role.
- The roles can be dynamically enabled or disabled.
- In order for the role to be effective-
    - a role must be created first
    - permissions must be assigned to a role
    - roles must be assigned to the logins

- the logins will enable the role

These steps are explained with an example-

Step 1: Creating a role

Syntax:`>create role role_name`

Example:`>create role sales_manager`

A role by name sales_manager is created and an entry is made into the syssrvroles system table found in master.

NOTE-Roles are server wide and they do not belong to a schema. That means there is no ownership for a role.

Step 2: To grant permission to a role.

Permission to a role must be granted within the database.

Example:

```
>use salesdb
>go
>grant insert on sales_table to sales manager
```

When the permission is granted within the database, the role information is also stored in a system table called sysroles within the database.

Step 3:Assigning role to a login

The roles must be assigned to a login from the master datbase. Ad explained earlier the role_login assignment information is stored in syssrvroles system table found in master.

```
>grant role sales_manager to abdul, mark
```

Step 4:

By default the roles are disabled. The user must enable the roles.

Example:

- Login to the server using login name.
- Then issue:

```
>set role <role_name> on
```

Another way is that the logins can be modified, so that the associated role can be automatically turned "ON" at the login time.

Example:

```
>sp_modifylogin abdul, "add default role", sales_manager
```

Now the role sales manager role is automatically enabled while connecting to the server.

To display user defined role information, use the system procedure sp_displayroles.

Example:

```
>sp_displayroles abdul
```

To list the currently active roles, use:

```
>sp_activeroles
```

Dropping a role:

Syntax:

```
>drop role role_name
```

Roles can be dropped by logins with SSO_roles. All the permissions granted to the role must be revoked prior to dropping a role.

Alternatively, issue:

Drop role role_name with override permissions granted to the role in all the databases are automatically removed and then the role is dropped.

Precedence of permission:

Role permission always have higher precedence than the user permission.

Example: Within the database salesdb, a database user has a permission insert on table sales_table. The same database user also has a permission to insert on table sales_table because of the association of the role sales_manager with the login.

Now if the insert permission is revoked from the database user, the user can still insert into table sales_table. Because the insert permission is also associated with the role sales_manager, role permissions take the higher precedence.

CHAPTER - 6

DATABASE OBJECTS AND THEIR MANAGEMENT IN SYBASE ASE

Overview Database objects are the fundamental building blocks within Sybase Adaptive Server Enterprise (ASE) that help structure and manage data. These objects include tables, indexes, views, triggers, stored procedures, and more. Understanding and efficiently managing these objects is crucial for database administrators to maintain data integrity, optimize performance, and support application requirements.

Tables

Tables are the primary structures that store data in rows and columns. Each table is defined by a set of columns, where each column has a specific data type. Creating a table involves defining its schema and specifying constraints to enforce data integrity.

To create a new table, the CREATE TABLE statement is used.

For example:

```
CREATE TABLE employees(
employee_id INT PRIMARY KEY,
```

```
first_name VARCHAR(50),
last_name VARCHAR(50),
birth_date DATE,
hire_date DATE,
salary DECIMAL(10, 2));
```

In this example, the employees table is created with columns for employee ID, first name, last name, birth date, hire date, and salary. The employee_id column is defined as the primary key.

Constraints are rules enforced on table columns to ensure data integrity. Common constraints include primary key, foreign key, unique, check, and not null.

Indexes

Indexes improve the performance of query operations by providing quick access paths to data. They are especially useful for large tables where full table scans would be inefficient.

The CREATE INDEX statement creates an index on one or more columns of a table. For example:

```
CREATE INDEX idx_last_name ON employees (last_name);
```

This statement creates an index on the last_name column of the employees table, improving the performance of queries that filter by last name.

There are two types of indexes: clustered and non-clustered.

Clustered indexes determine the physical order of data in the table, while non-clustered indexes provide a logical order without altering the physical order.

Views

Views are virtual tables that provide a way to present data from one or more tables. They can simplify complex queries, enhance security by limiting data access, and provide a consistent interface to underlying tables.

The CREATE VIEW statement defines a new view.

For example:

```
CREATE VIEW employee_details
AS
SELECT    employee_id,    first_name,    last_name,
department_name
FROM employees
JOIN departments ON
employees.department_id = departments.department_id;
```

This view, employee_details, combines data from the employees and departments tables.

Triggers, Stored Procedures, and User-Defined Functions

Triggers are special types of stored procedures that automatically execute in response to certain events on a table, such as INSERT, UPDATE, or DELETE operations. They are used to enforce business rules, maintain audit trails, and ensure data consistency.

Stored procedures are precompiled collections of SQL statements that perform a specific task. They can accept input parameters, return output parameters, and encapsulate business logic.

User-defined functions (UDFs) are similar to stored procedures but can be used in SQL expressions. They return a single value and can simplify complex calculations and logic.

Efficient management of database objects in Sybase ASE is essential for maintaining data integrity, optimizing performance, and supporting application requirements. By understanding and utilizing tables, indexes, views, triggers, stored procedures, and user-defined functions, database administrators can ensure a robust and scalable database environment.

CHAPTER – 7
SYSTEM RECOVERY PROCESS

OVERVIEW

The term recovery is commonly misunderstood, and it is often always associated with restoring a damaged database due to media failures from a previously stored backup copy. In fact, recovery refers to:

- Automatic recovery due to instance failure or shutdown.
- Media recovery

In this chapter we shall understand the automatic recovery process that the Adaptive server has to perform in order to protect the server from power failures and computer failures. However, automatic recovery is not a solution for media failures. To protect against media failures, you need to regularly backup the databases.

RECOVERY

Recovery is a process of restoring the databases to the transaction consistent state after a server shutdown.

Alternatively Adaptive server automatic recovery process is a mechanism of synchronizing the log with the database when the server is started.

TRANSACTION

A transaction is defined as a logical unit of work which is either completely done or completely not done. All the transactions are "atomic" in nature. All the transactions modify data in the database. The transaction begins with one or more DML statements and end with a transaction control statement such as commit or rollback.

The transaction log

The adaptive server uses transaction logs to keep track of all database modifications. The adaptive server transaction log is nothing but "syslogs" system table. Every database has its own "syslogs" system table. The syslogs system table is created in the logsegment of every database.

To view the tables of the logsegment use the system procedure:

```
>sp_helpsegment "logsegment"
```

The logsegment of every database contains only "syslogs" table and no other tables are stored by the logsegment.

The transaction log is always a write ahead log. When a transaction modifies the database, the adaptive server writes the modifications to the log. Once all the changes are recorded into the log, then the modification is done to the data page in the memory.

If the transaction is incomplete then the adaptive server reverses all the modifications made by the transaction. The Adaptive server uses the transaction records in the "syslogs" table to perform rollback

Transaction modes

The transactions are executed either in **chained mode** or in **unchained mode**.

In a chained mode transaction, the server automatically executes an implicit begin transaction before executing DML statements. However, an explicit commit work or rollback work is needed to end the transaction.

In unchained mode transactions, the transactions are always defined explicitly with "begin transaction" statement, and the transaction should be committed explicitly with end transaction statements. Note that the choice of using chained mode or unchained mode of transaction is purely an application design decision. The adaptive server by default uses unchained transaction mode.

To view the current transaction mode

```
>select @@tranchained
```

Transaction Control statements

The automic transactions are started with Begin transaction command

Begin transaction or begin tran - marks the beginning of the transaction.

Commit transaction or commit tran – marks the end of a transaction and the database changes are permanent.

Rollback transaction or rollback tran – the server marks the end of a transaction and aborts all the changes.

Here is an example-

```
>begin tran tran 1
>change 1
>change 2
>commit tran
```

The above transaction is a single transaction containing multiple statements.

Nested Transaction and log behavior

The transaction commands can be nested inside each other. That means a transaction begins with a begin tran statement. Without using commit statement or rollback statement if another transaction is started, then automatically the two transactions are nested.

Example:

```
>begin tran tran1
>change 1
>begin tran tran2
>change 2
```

In the above example the first transaction has not completed and it is still active and the application has started the second transaction.

@@ trancount

The adaptive server keeps track of the nesting level of the transaction using a global variable called @@trancount.

The nested transaction and the value held by the @@trancount variable and the log writing behavior is explained with an example.

Example:

```
>begin tran tran1
>change 1
>begin tran tran2
>change 2
>commit tran
>commit tran
```

- When the first transaction is started, the “begin tran tran1” information is recorded in the log page and the @@transaction variable is incremented by 1. This means the beginning of the transaction.

Log page

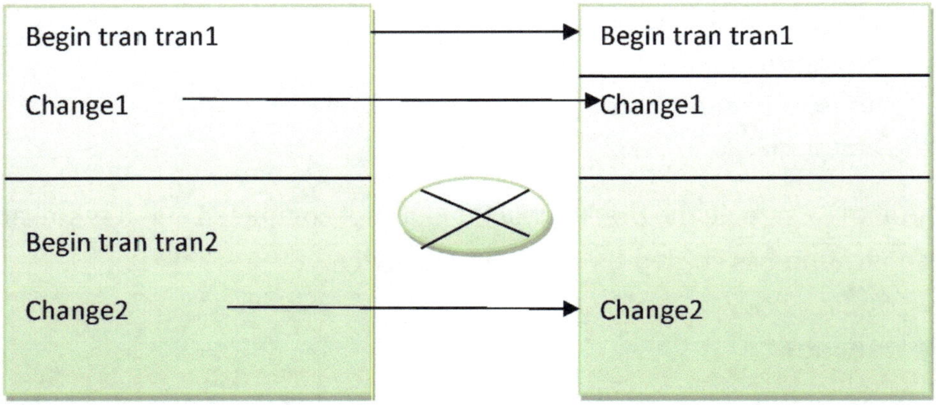

- However, when the second transaction "begin tran tra2" is started, it is not recorded in the transaction log page but only the @@trancount variable is incremented by 1.

```
>select @@trancount
```

@@trancount shows a value 2.

- Now when the inner nested transaction is committed, the server merely decrements the @@trancount value by 1, but the inner nested transaction is actually not committed. This means that the entire transaction (inner nested transaction and the outer non-nested transaction) are still active.

Only when the outer non-nested transaction is committed, the @@trancount value will hold zero. Now the server commits the entire work and writes "end transaction with commit" into the transaction log page.

Log page

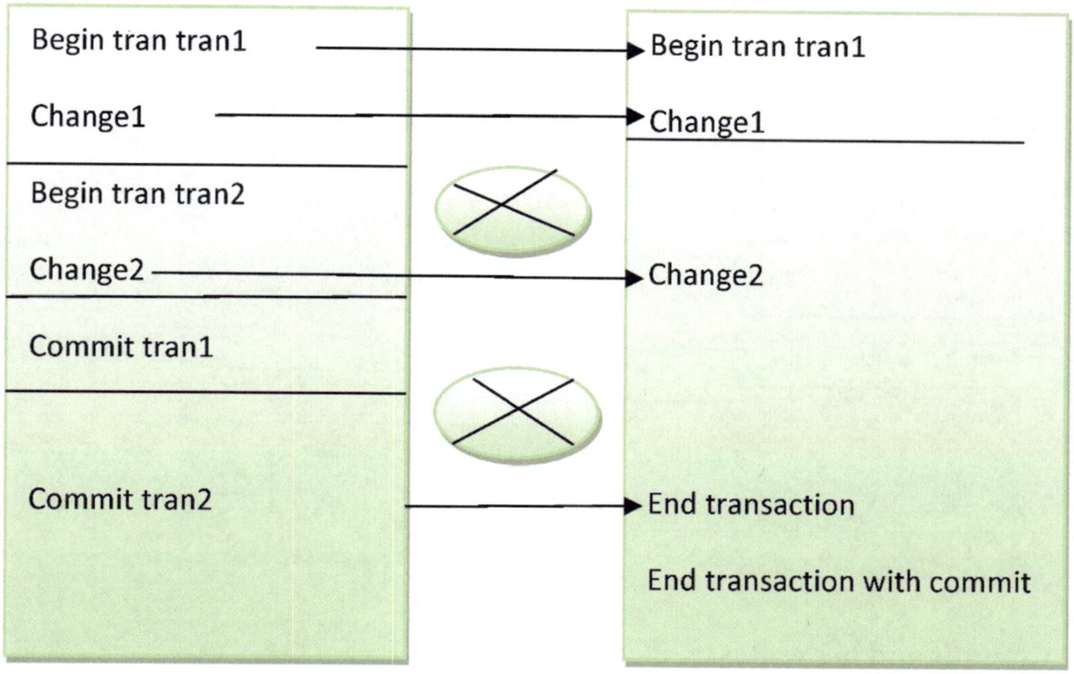

You can observe that even though the application is performing multiple transactions in the form of nested transaction, from the database perspective, it is just a single transaction.

It is only the final commit statement which completes the entire work and changes to the database are permanent. If a final commit statement is missed, the variable @@trancount will hold a non-zero value, and the server considers the transaction as active. So the transaction is considered incomplete. The simplest way to interpret is that if @@trancount is a non-zero value, the transaction is incomplete and if @@trancount value is zero, the transaction is completed.

However, the same is not true with respect to rollback transaction. Irrespective of the nesting level and @@trancount value, a single rollback statement is enough to rollback all the transactions. When the server encounters a rollback statement, the @@trancount value is reset to zero and the server records a "end transaction with abort", statement into the transaction log.

Log page

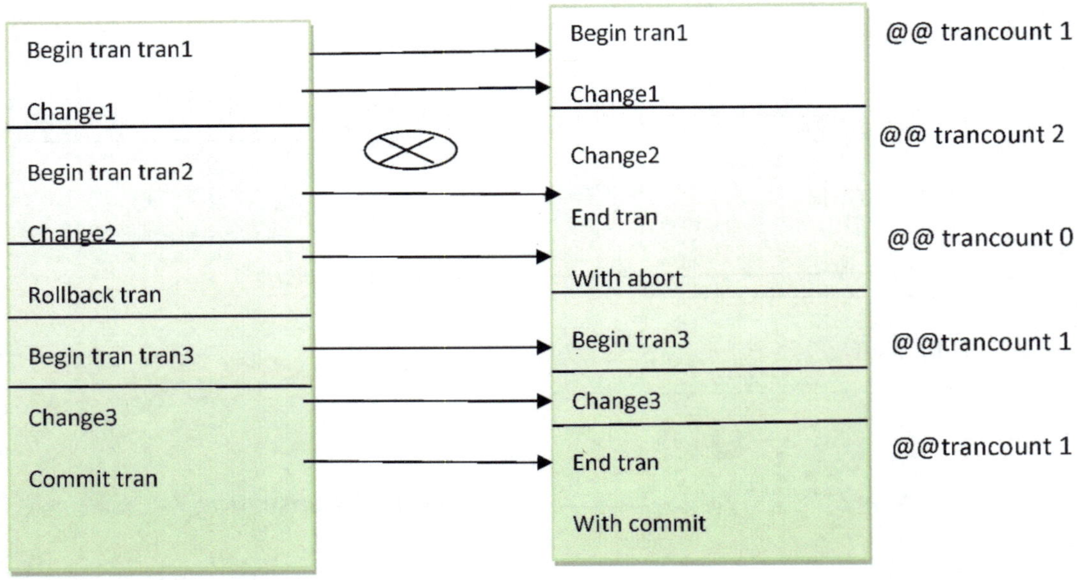

Commit and log writes

When an application performs a transaction, the adaptive server reads the data pages into data cache(or the data pages may already been cached into memory). Then the data pages are modified. The modified data pages are called *dirty pages.*

Before modifying the data pages, the server processes the log records. Incidentally, the log records are also processed in the data cache.

When the application issues a commit, the server writes a "end transaction with commit" into the log page and immediately the log page is written to the disk(log segment of the database). At no point of time the log pages will be stored in memory when the transaction is committed. This will simply ensure that the data modification are preserved in the database and protects the committed work. On the other hand, if the log pages were allowed to remain in data cache without writing into the disk, a completed transaction could be lost if the server were to fail unexpectedly. So it is to be noted that transaction commit statements will immediately trigger log page writes to the database.

In addition to this event, the log pages will also be written to the database when the cache is full or when hundred rows are recorded into the log page or when the server issues a checkpoint.

Data page writes

On the other hand, the adaptive server always tries to retain data pages in database memory, so that frequent physical reads from the disk are avoided.

The data pages will be displaced from data cache memory only when the adaptive server needs space to read other databases.

The dirty pages are written to the disk during checkpoint process.

CHECKPOINT

Checkpoint is a server event which causes the modified data pages, index pages and the log pages to be written to the database.

Checkpoints are primarily issued to reduce the work of the server at the recovery time. Checkpoints reduce the recovery time and bring up the server faster. The following events will take place when the checkpoint is issued.

- The dirty log pages are copied to the disk.(write ahead logs)
- The dirty data pages and index pages are written to the disk.
- A check point record is entered to the log.

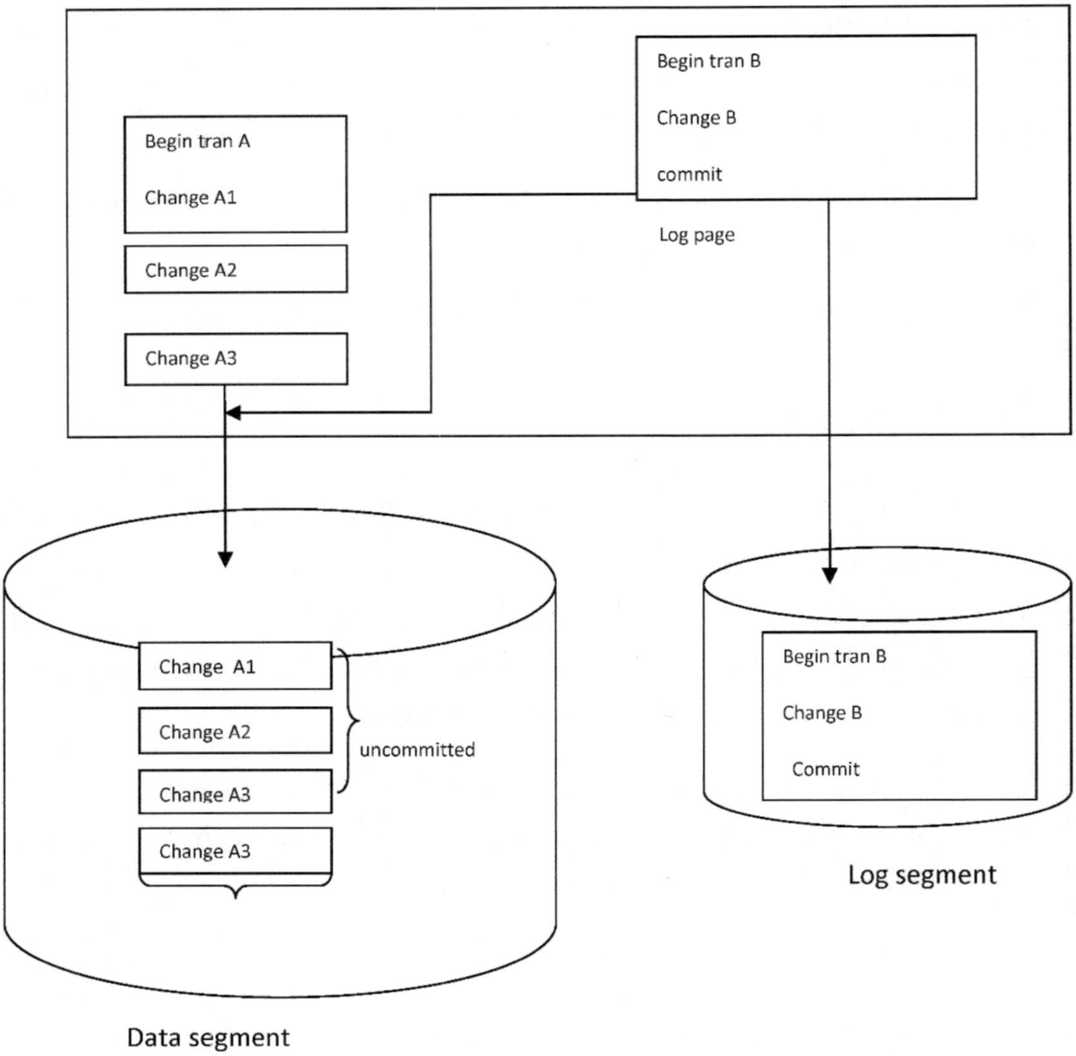

Note that the checkpoint process will write both committed and uncommitted modified data to the data segment. Whereas commit will write only the log page to the log segment.

The checkpoint records will also be entered into the transaction logs. This checkpoint record will help the server to identify the incomplete transaction during the recovery process.

Recovery Process

The recovery process ensures that the databases are in the transaction consistent state. It should not be understood that the recovery process is performed only during server failures. Automatic recovery is performed every time the server is restarted and the recovery is dependent on the checkpoint as well.

The following tasks are performed during automatic recovery:

- The server locates the most recent check point in the transaction log.
- The server creates a list of active transactions at the time of checkpoint.
- The transaction log page is compared with data pages of the database.
- Modifications due to committed transactions are verified with log page and if necessary, the changes are reapplied.
- Modifications in the data page due to incomplete or rollback transaction are removed from the data pages.
- The server writes fresh checkpoint information into the transaction log so that the next recovery starts from the new checkpoint rather than from the beginning of the log. As you could see that the recovery process also places a checkpoint. This is very significant because the recovery no longer compares the entire log, but only a part of the log since the last checkpoint.

Recovering incomplete and committed transactions is explained in the following section with example.

When the server is up and running, there might be several transactions in progress. So when the server shuts down intermittently, some transactions may have been completed and some transactions may be incomplete. Hence the sever should store sufficient information to restore each database to a transaction consistent state.

Scenario 1 : Redo as Roll forward complete transactions

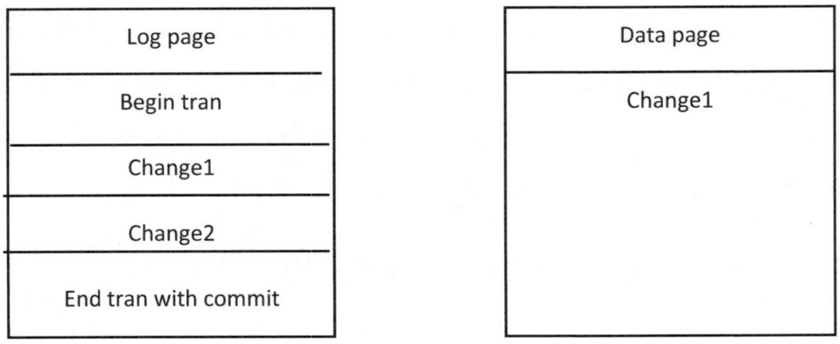

For all committed transactions, the log page on the disk will contain a "begin tran" record and an "end transaction with commit" record. When the server encounters this, there are two possibilities.

The respective data page may contain the modified data. In this case there is no need to apply the modifications from the log page.

The data page may not contain modified data. In this case, the modifications are applied from the log page to the data page. It is called "Roll forward" activity.

Scenario 2: Undo or Roll back

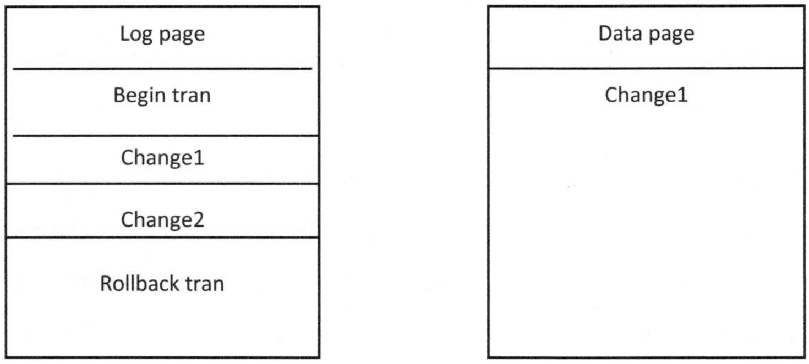

For all the transactions will rollback statement or incomplete transactions, the log page on the disk will contain a "begin transaction" record and an "end transaction with abort" record.

When the server encounters this log page again, there are two possibilities that may occur.

- The respective data page may contain the modifications. The adaptive server removes the modifications and restores with the data prior to modification. This activity is called "Roll back" or "undo".
- The respective data page may not contain the modifications. In this case no need to change the contents of the data page

Execution of checkpoints

The system administrator and database owners can initiate checkpoints on the database.

Syntax: checkpoint

The following user initiated events cause a checkpoint.

- Changing the database option using sp_dboption
- Performing backup of a database and back up of transaction log.
- Shutting down the adaptive server using wait option.

In addition to user initiated checkpoints the server also periodically issues checkpoints.

Housekeeper task:

The system process housekeeper performs write operation of dirty pages from memory to the disk.

During the adaptive server's idle time, it activates the housekeeper task to flush out buffer pools in the cache. Apart from this the housekeeper also "wakes up" the checkpoint server task. Then the "checkpoint task" will determine whether to perform a checkpoint or not, based on the number of log records generated since the previous checkpoint. If there are more than 100 log records it issues a checkpoint..

The checkpoints issued as a result of housekeeper tasks are called *free checkpoints.*

Recovery Interval checkpoint

The amount of time required by the adaptive server to recover a database is directly proportional to the number of unrecovered transactions in the log.

If there are very less modifications since the last checkpoint, the database will be recovered in very less time.

If there are a large number of unrecovered log records to be processed, then the database recovery time will also be more. This can be problematic as startup time.

You can configure the recovery time of a database using the parameter "Recovery interval in minutes".

To view the configured value and default value, use:

```
>sp_configure "recovery interval in minutes"
>go
```

The default value is 5 minutes, i.e, each database will be recovered within the maximum estimated time of 5 minutes. The setting of "recovery interval in minutes" parameter has a bearing on the Checkpoint Frequency.

The adaptive server pre-computes the checkpoint frequency based on the "recovery interval in minutes" parameter.

In simpler words, if the recovery time interval is less, then the server executes more frequent checkpoints. This affects server performance. Because by initiating checkpoints more frequently, you will be causing more frequent physical writes to the disk.

Longer the recovery time interval, the server issues less frequent checkpoints.

Database Recovery order

During server startup, the system databases are recovered first and then the user databases. The recovery order for the system databases are:

- master database
- sybsystemdb
- model
- tempdb (dropped and recreated)

- sybsystemprocs
- sybsecurity (if created)

The user databases are recovered by default in the order of their "dbid".

User can connect to the server once all the system databases are recovered. But the user cannot access a given database until that database has been restored completely and it is online.

Setting the database recovery order.

You can prioritize the database recovery order using the system procedure.

```
>sp_dbrecovery_order
```

Example:

```
>exec sp_dbrecovery_order salesdb, 1
>exec sp_dbrecovery_order testdb, 2
```

After the system databases have been recovered, the salesdb will be recovered first followed by testdb database. Other databases will be recovered as per their "dbid".

CHAPTER – 8
BACKUP AND RECOVERY

OVERVIEW

In any organization, periodic backing up of your business related data is one of the most mechanical tasks you perform. But it may also be the important task! In the general practice, backup refers to the copying and archiving of your data, so that it may be used to restore after a data loss.

Primarily, backups have two different purposes. Their primary purpose is to recover data. The data loss may be due to accidental deletion of data or due to corruption.

Another purpose of backups is to recover data to a prior point in time as per the user defined retention policy. The system administrators need to analyze what needs to be backed up so that they can develop an effective backup strategy and automate them.

In essence, backups need to be performed in order to be protected against:

- media failures
- machine failures
- site failures and to
- recover data due to application error

The backups need to be tested under simulated disaster conditions and the recovery methods must be well documented.

Backup Basics

A database backup or database dump is a physical copy of the entire database.

A database "load" restores the database from a dump device.

When we perform restoration, the basic unit of recovery is a "database". That means entire database is restored, and it is not possible to restore a part of a database. Sybase does not allow physical backup at the table level. Also you cannot copy the files at the operating system level as a backup copy.

TYPE OF BACKUPS

Full Database backup: We perform a backup of entire database, i.e, both the data segments and log segments are backed up.

When the databases are built with "mixed log and data", you cannot perform backup of only the log segment.

Also when the database option "trunc log on chkpt" is true, and when performing minimally logged operations, you need to perform full database backups.

Transaction log backup: You can perform backup of only transaction log. Transaction log backup is possible only when the data segments and log segment are separated.

Up to the minute recovery and point in time recovery are possible only with the valid transaction log backups.

Take a look at the following scenario to understand the difference between relying on full database backups and additionally taking transaction log backups.

Backup Scenario 1

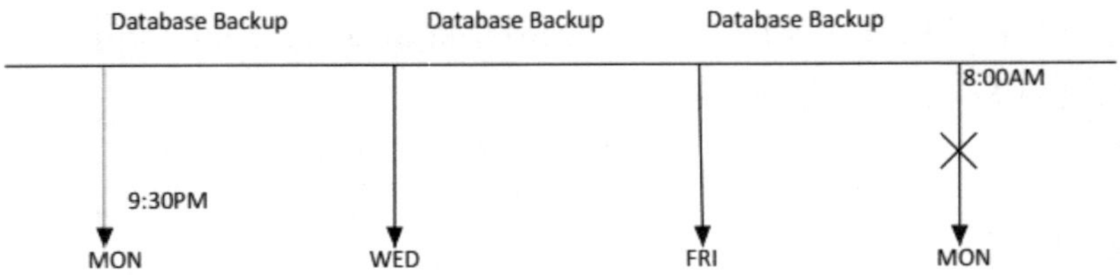

- The database is created with "mixed log and data"
- Full database backup is scheduled on alternative days at 9:30 pm in the night.
- Device failure is reported on Monday at 8:00 pm.

Restoration: In this scenario, since transaction log backups are not possible, you can restore the database from the most recent backup and the most recent backup happens to be on Friday. So you can restore data till Friday and the business work from Friday to Monday 8:00pm could not be recovered. The restoration point is the most recent backup and up to the minute recovery is not possible.

Backup Scenario 2

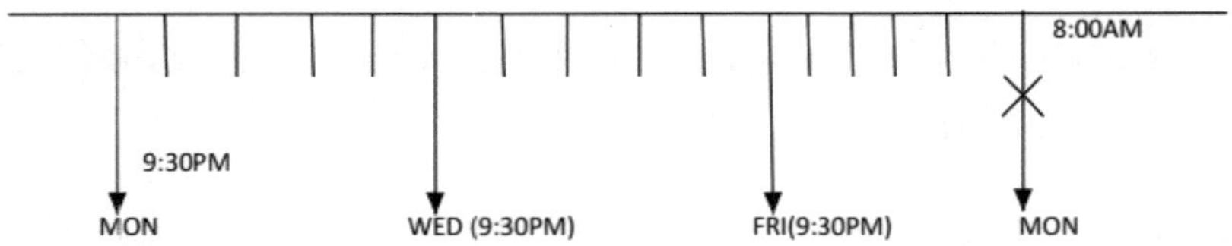

- The database is created by separating the data segment from the log segment and the log segment is on its own device. This allows for taking full database backup as well as transaction log backup.
- The backup strategy is to take full database backup on alternative days. Transaction log backup is performed every one hour cycle.
- The database failure is reported at 8:00 am on Monday.
- The most recent full database backup is performed on Friday and the last transaction log backup is on Monday 7:00 am.

Restoration: In this scenario, you can restore the database by using the most recent backup on Friday. Since you have valid transaction log backups from Friday to Monday 7:00 am, you can apply the transaction log backups since Friday and recover the transactions up to 7:00 am on Monday.

- If the device failure is not that of the log segment, you can still take a special log dump(explained later) and you can recover complete transactions up to the point of failure. This is called as up to the minute recovery. Up to the minute recovery is only possible with transaction log backups.

BACKUP SERVER

Backup server is an open server application which is running on the same machine as Adaptive server. The backup server completely bypasses the adaptive server processes and it directly accesses the database devices to perform dump and load, Hence it does not interfere with the data processing and do not degrade the server performance.

Backup Server Features

- Database dumps can be created when the users are active.
- The backup server manages I/O, rather than using Adaptive server resources.
- Platform specific tape handing options are supported.
- Multiple database dumps and transaction log dumps can be stored in a single tape.
- You can perform "multi stripe dumps". This option allows you to split the database into almost equal portions and perform backup of each portion into a separate device. The dump striping option allows you to use up to 32 backup devices simultaneously.
- Dump and loads can be performed over a network using a remote backup server running on another machine.
- Since Version 12.5 and later, dump and load can be performed for a large page server.
- i,e a backup performed on a server with 4k page can be restored on a server with 4k page
- Backup can be compressed.

Backup Server Architecture

Backup server is needed to perform database backup(dump) and to load databases.

The transaction log dump and load is also performed by Backup server.

A backup server is an instance running on the host machine, where the adaptive server is running.

The following figure depicts the fundamentals of backup server.

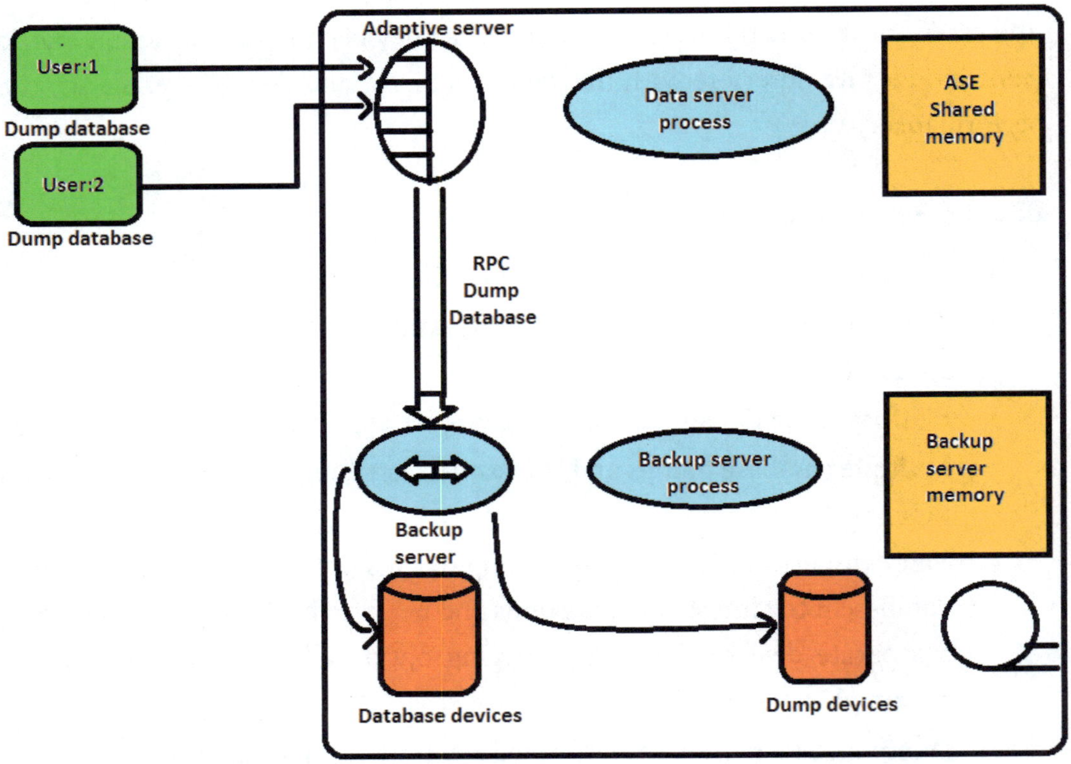

Backup server was completely re-architected since ASE Version 12.0. The major enhancements are:

- Asynchronous data transfer
- Large page support and dump compression
- Increased size of I/O operations and thereby reducing the I/O calls.
- Using larger network I/O.

Configuring Backup server server using Resource file

In UNIX environment, you can build a backup server using the resource file srvbuild.backupserver.

Path: $SYBASE/$SYBASE_ASE/init/sample_resource_files

Procedure: Copy the resource file srvbuild.backupserver for customization and make the following entries.

Example:

```
$ cp srvbuild.backupserver.rs test_backupserver.rs
```

Edit the file test_backupserver and add the entries for:

- Name of the backup server
- Hostname
- Portnumber
- Name of the adaptive server(optional) and password for sa(optional)

```
sybinit.release_directory: USE_DEFAULT
sybinit.product: bsrv
bsrv.server_name: backup_server
bsrv.new_config: yes
bsrv.do_add_backup_server: yes
bsrv.do_upgrade: no
bsrv.network_protocol_list: tcp
bsrv.network_hostname_list: localhost
bsrv.network_port_list: 7000
bsrv.language: USE_DEFAULT
bsrv.character_set: USE_DEFAULT
bsrv.tape_config_file: USE_DEFAULT
bsrv.errorlog: USE_DEFAULT
sqlsrv.related_sqlsrvr: adaptive_server_name
sqlsrv.sa_login: sa
sqlsrv.sa_password: USE_DEFAULT
```

Issue srvbuildres command to build the backup server.

```
$ srvbuildres -r test_backupserver.rs
```

```
Building Backup Server 'backup_server':
Writing entry into directory services...
Directory services entry complete.
Writing RUN_backup_server file...
RUN_backup_server file complete.
Starting server...
Server started.
Setting server name in Adaptive Server...
Server name added.
Server 'backup_server' was successfully created.
```

Verify the backup server process using "showserver" command or using any OS commands.

How a Backup server works

Basically no language handlers are installed in the backup server and hence you cannot run any commands directly within the backup server. You can just establish a connection to the backup server using isql utility, but you cannot run any commands.

To perform a backup of a user or a system database you need to:

- Connect to the adaptive server.

  ```
  >isql -Usa -STEST
  >password:
  ```

- Verify whether the backup server has been listed in the sysservers system table found in master database using the system procedure:

```
>sp_helpserver

name                  network_name
         security_mechanism
         server_principal           class
         status
         id cost
      -------------------- ----------------------------
      ----------------------------------------
```

```
    ---------------------------------- ---------------------
-
    ----------------------------------------------------------
----------------------------------------------------------
----
    ---- -------
SYB_BACKUP                    TEST_BS
        NULL
        NULL                  ASEnterprise
        timeouts, no net password encryption, writable ,
enable login redirection
        1        NULL
        Test                  Test
        NULL
        NULL                  local
        0        0
(return status = 0)
```

- If the backup server is not listed, you need to make an entry for the backup server, using the system procedure sp_addserver

Example:

```
>sp_addserver SYB_BACKUP, NULL, TEST_BS
```

```
Adding server 'SYB_BACKUP', physical name 'TEST_BS'
Server added.
(return status = 0)
```

- Then you need to issue the dump database command.

Example:

```
>dump database database_name
>to 'path_file_name'

>dump database master to
>'/home/backup/master_full.dmp'
```

```
WARNING: In order to LOAD the master database, the ASE must run
in single-user
mode. If the master database dump uses multiple volumes, you must
execute
sp_volchanged on another ASE at LOAD time in order to signal volume
changes.
Backup Server session id is: 5. Use this value when executing the
'sp_volchanged' system stored procedure after fulfilling any
volume change
request from the Backup Server.
Backup Server: 4.41.1.1: Creating new disk file
/opt/sybase/master_full.dmp.
Backup Server: 6.28.1.1: Dumpfile name 'master1405109E09 ' section
number 1
mounted on disk file '/opt/sybase/master_full.dmp'
Backup Server: 4.188.1.1: Database master: 1368 kilobytes (26%)
DUMPed.
Backup Server: 4.188.1.1: Database master: 5146 kilobytes (100%)
DUMPed.
Backup Server: 3.43.1.1: Dump phase number 1 completed.
Backup Server: 3.43.1.1: Dump phase number 2 completed.
Backup Server: 3.43.1.1: Dump phase number 3 completed.
Backup Server: 4.188.1.1: Database master: 5154 kilobytes (100%)
DUMPed.
Backup Server: 3.42.1.1: DUMP is complete (database master).
```

- When the user issues a dump database command, the Adaptive server instructs the backup server through remote procedure calls to backup a specific database.
- The backup server does not use the resources of Adaptive server, rather the Backup server directly handles I/0.
- The backup server is allocated a shared memory directly from the operating system and it does not use the shared memory allocated to the Adaptive server.
- The backup server uses its own threads and it reads the used pages of the target database and performs backup.
- The backup server creates a dump device and messages are sent to the session which initiated the backup.

Configuring memory and threads for the Backup server

The backup server startup script is automatically created when the backup server is created. The default name is RUN_<BACKUP_SERVER>

Path: **$SYBASE/$SYBASE_ASE/install**

As discussed, the backup server uses its own resources to perform dump and load. By default the backup server is allocated a memory of 48M and it uses a default number of 48 service threads. You can specify the maximum amount of shared memory and service threads in the backup server startup script RUN_<Backup_server>.

In order to increase the shared memory of the backup server use -m option.

To increase the number of service threads use -P option.

Example:

```
#!/bin/sh
#
# Error log path:/opt/sybase/ASE-15_0/install/Test_bkp.log
# Maximum number of network connections:25
# Maximum number of server connections:20
# Multibuf executable path:/opt/sybase/ASE-15_0/bin/sybmultbuf
# Backup Server name:Test_bkp
#
/opt/sybase/ASE-15_0/bin/backupserver \
-e/opt/sybase/ASE-15_0/install/Test_bkp.log \
-N25 \
-C20 \
-M/opt/sybase/ASE-15_0/bin/sybmultbuf \
-STest_bkp \
-m60 \
-P60
```

Configuring higher value of shared memory and service threads is needed when performing multiple stripe dumps and load.

The backup server allocates memory to each stripe. The memory per stripe is calculated by dividing the total amount of configured shared memory by the configured number of service threads.

Example: Total configured memory is 1024MB.
The number of configured service threads is 128.
The memory per stripe would be 8MB per stripe.

The backup server needs a minimum shared memory of 128 KB for the stripe. If we monotonically increase the number of service threads without proportionally increasing the shared memory, then the backup server may not start up because of insufficient memory.

Start up and Shutdown a Backup server

The backup server is started just like the way we start the adaptive server. Use startserver command to start the backup server.

Example:

```
>path:$SYBASE/$SYBASE_ASE/install
>startserver -f RUN_<BACKUP_server>
```

To shutdown the backup server, login to the adaptive server where the backup server is listed in the sysservers system table and issue:

```
>shutdown
>SYB_BACKUP
>go
```

The default shutdown option is with wait. This option allows the backup server to complete the current dump and load operations and then the backup server is shutdown gracefully. However, no new backup requests are permitted.

The other shutdown option is with no wait, which immediately terminates the backup server process even if there is a dump or load operation progress.

Remote or Backup server

If there is a requirement to access the media on a separate hardware and to perform dump and load on a remote server, we need a Remote backup server. The local backup server can only access the disk or tape drives which are physically installed on the same machine where the backup server and adaptive server is running.

Consider using a Remote backup server if many Adaptive servers are on different host machines and each one of them need to use a remote backup server on a networked dump host. But note that local backup servers perform better than remote backup server. A local backup server is always needed even if you are taking backups through a remote backup server. The communication to the remote backup server must be coordinated by the local backup server. Using remote procedure calls, the local backup server passes the backup and load requests and the data to the remote backup server.

Identifying the Local and Remote Backup servers

When a dump or load command is issued at the Adaptive server, the Adaptive server looks for a SYB_BACKUP entry in the master..sysservers system table. SYB_BACKUP is a logical name which is mapped to the physical Backup server. Then using the entry for a service name, port number in the interface file , the Adaptive server connects to the Backup server., i.e, the Adaptive server acts as a client to the Backup server.

To identify the Remote Backup server, it must be added into the interface file. The remote backup server name must be referred to in the dump and load commands.

Example:

```
>dump database database_name
>to "path_file_name"
>at Remote_Backup_SERVER_NAME
```

Also the adaptive server must be configured for remote access. This is done by using the configuration parameter " allow remote access"

Example:

```
>sp_configure "allow remote access", 1
```

```
Parameter Name

        Default           Memory Used         Config Value
        Run Value         Unit
```

```
        Type
      --------------------------------------------------------
--
      --------------------- ---------------------- ------------
-----------
      ----------------------- -----------------------------
------
      --------------------
allow remote access
                 1                 0                 1
                 1                 switch
dynamic
(1 row affected)
Configuration option changed. ASE need not be rebooted since the
option is
dynamic.
Resulting configuration value and memory use have not changed from
previous
values: new configuration value 1, previous value 1.
(return status = 0)
```

The default option is 1 (on) and this configuration option is dynamic.

Roles and permissions

By default the database owner DBO, has the permissions to perform dump and load of a database and these permissions are not grantable by DBO to other users of the database. However, any user who is aliased as the DBO can use dump and load commands within the database.

The SSO user can grant role oper_role to any login. The logins who has been granted with the oper_role role can perform backup of any database at the server level and the operator need not be the user of the database.

DUMP DATABASE COMMAND

The dump database command makes a backup copy of the entire database including the transaction log.

Syntax:

```
dump database database_name
        to [compress::[compression_level::]]stripe_device
            [at backup_server_name]
            [density = density_value,
            blocksize = number_bytes,
            capacity = number_kilobytes,
            dumpvolume = volume_name,
            file = file_name]
            with verify[= header | full]
        [stripe on [compress::[compression_level::]]stripe_device
            [at backup_server_name]
            [density = density_value,
            blocksize = number_bytes,
            capacity = number_kilobytes,
            dumpvolume = volume_name,
            file = file_name]]
            [[stripe on [compress::[compression_level::]]stripe_device
            [at backup_server_name]
            [density = density_value,
            blocksize = number_bytes,
            capacity = number_kilobytes,
            dumpvolume = volume_name,
            file = file_name]]...]
        [with {
            density = density_value,
```

```
blocksize = number_bytes,
capacity = number_kilobytes,
compression = compress_level
dumpvolume = volume_name,
file = file_name,
[dismount | nodismount],
[nounload | unload],
passwd = password,
retaindays = number_days,
[noinit | init],
notify = {client | operator_console}
}]
```

For the complete explanation of the dump database command refer the Sybase reference manual documentation.

The following examples represent different ways of using dump database command.

Specifying a dump device

You can take a database dump by specifying the absolute path, relative path or by using a logical name for the dump device.

Example:

```
>dump database test to "/usr/backups/usr_full.dmp"
```

```
Backup Server session id is: 9. Use this value when executing the
'sp_volchanged' system stored procedure after fulfilling any
volume change
request from the Backup Server.
Backup Server: 4.41.1.1: Creating new disk file
/usr/backups/usr_full.dmp.
Backup Server: 6.28.1.1: Dumpfile name 'ma1405109EB4 ' section
number 1
mounted on disk file '/usr/backups/usr_full.dmp'
Backup Server: 4.188.1.1: Database ma: 812 kilobytes (100%)
DUMPed.
Backup Server: 3.43.1.1: Dump phase number 1 completed.
Backup Server: 3.43.1.1: Dump phase number 2 completed.
```

```
Backup Server: 4.188.1.1: Database ma: 816 kilobytes (100%) DUMPed.
Backup Server: 3.43.1.1: Dump phase number 3 completed.
Backup Server: 4.188.1.1: Database ma: 820 kilobytes (100%) DUMPed.
Backup Server: 3.42.1.1: DUMP is complete (database ma).
```

For a dump database command the percentage information represents estimation of completion of backup based on the total size of the database.

Example: To specify the relative path in the dump database command

```
>dump database test to "test_full.dmp"
```

The backup server resolves the relative path file name and the database dump is placed on the current directory.

You can use the logical name for a dump device by using the system procedure sp_addump device. It simply maps the absolute path of the file to a logical name and it is listed in the sysdevices system table.

Example:

```
>sp_addumpdevice "disk", "disk_dev", "/usr/backups/database.dmp"
```

Use the dump database command with logical name.

```
>dump database test to "disk.dev"
```

However, you cannot use the logical name when performing backups using Remote backup server. You must use the absolute physical path.

Backing databases to a tape device

You can perform backups to either tape devices or to disk files. You can backup a single database or many databases into a single tape device. Also you can backup single database to multiple tape devices.

Using tape devices as a dump device has the following benefits.

- tape backups are more secure

- manage multiple database dumps to a single tape device
- less sensitive to data changes

However,

- tape backups tend to be very slow
- tape backups need to be periodically tested.

Recommended practice is to perform primary backups to a disk device and then move the backup to tape device.

Example

```
>dump database test to dump_tape_dev
```

When the dump database command is issued, the backup server checks whether the device type is a tape or a disk device. If the device type is not known then the backup server checks the configuration file. If the configuration file is not found, the dump command fails.

Tape operations

The default non-rewinding functionality of the tape automatically positions the tape at the end of the tape data. The backup server writes end of file information at the end of every dump operation.

To perform a new backup, the backup server looks for a new end of file table and the tape is positioned forward and points to the next file. If the end of file information is not found, then the backup server automatically rewinds the tape.

Multiple dumps to a single tape

To place the multiple database dumps to a single tape device use the following procedure:

- Use with init option of the database command. This rewinds the tape to scan the initial position and performs forward scan.

Example:

```
>dump database test1
```

```
>to "/dev"dump_tape
>with init
```

- Use with nounload option of the dump database to take backup of other databases. This option avoids overwriting of the dump volumes within the tape device.

Example:

```
>dump database test2
>to "/dev/dump_tape"
>with nounload
```

- Use with unload option of the dump database to take backup of the last database. This option automatically rewinds the tape.

Example:

```
    >dump database test3
    >to "/dev/dump_tape"
>with unload
```

Dump compression

You can reduce the space requirements for archived databases by using compression option in the dump database command.

Example:

```
    >dump database test to "/backups/test_full.dmp"
>with compression=6
```

The compression level is between 0 to 9 and 100 or 101. For single digit compression level 0 means no compression and 9 represents highest level of compression. The compression level 100 is less CPU intensive and provides a faster compression than 101.

In general, the greater the compression number, the longer will be the time to perform a backup. Sybase uses its own native compression method.

Multiple dumps

Using "stripe on" option in the dump database command allows you to perform backup of single database on multiple dump devices. The backup server equally divides the database into the number of specified stripes and dumps are made concurrently on all the devices specified. This reduces the time required to dump an individual database.

However, while loading form multiple stripe dumps you need to specify all the stripes and in the same order as you mentioned while backup the database.

Example:

```
>dump database test to '/backup/test_sd.dmp'
>stripe on '/backup/test_s2.dmp'
>stripe on '/backup/test_s3.dmp'
```

Password protected dumps:

You can protect your database dumps from unauthorized database loads by specifying the password parameter in the dump database command. When you load a database with a password protected dump, the backup server prompts for password and you must specify the valid password for the load operation to proceed.

Example:

```
      >dump database test to ".backup/test.d"
>with passwd = "test@3201"
```

You cannot specify the password parameter for transaction log dumps.

Improving Backup server performance

To improve the performance of dump and load commands, you can configure the backup server to use higher memory. This is done by using -m option in the in the RUN FILE and restart the backup server.

You can set the maximum number of the service threads using -P option in the RUN FILE and restarting the Backup server. Higher value of service threads is required when you are performing a multi stripe dump.

The default value of network connection that a backup server can initiate is 25. You need to increase the number of network connections by specifying the -N option of the backup server RUN FILE and restart the backup server. This is particularly required if you are performing multi stripe dumps initiated through a remote backup server.

Loading the Database

The load database command is primarily used to restore a database from a backup dump device. The restoration process will replace everything in the target database with the contents of the dump device, so that the original contents of the target database are lost.

To perform a load operation, the target database must exist. You can load the database dump to a existing database or you can create new database using for load option.

The size of the target database must be equal to or greater than the size of the source database where information is recorded in the dump device. In order to read the metadata information such as name of the source database, DBID, number pages, etc, issue:

```
>load database <database_name> from '<file name'
with headeronly
```

The load database command immediately sets the database status to "offline" in the sysdatabses system table. As a result, the database will be "offline" and all the users including the one who performed the load operation will not be able to access the database after the load operation.

This is because while performing the database dump, the server issues checkpoint on the database. The checkpoint process would write all the modified pages from memory to the database. The modified pages may have committed data as well as uncommitted data. So when you are performing dump,, the backup is always in transaction inconsistent mode.

While restoring the database, the load database command restores all used pages from the dump device into the target database. So the target database will also be in transaction inconsistent state.

To bring the database to the online state use the command:

```
>online database <database_name>
```

The online database process will initiate the recovery of syslogs table to ensure consistency and all the uncommitted actions are rolled back. Once the database is brought back to transaction consistent state, the database would be online and now it is accessible by all the users.

The load database process copies all the used pages into the target database. This means that if the database size of the dumped database is 10GB and the used pages are actually 2GB, then the used pages amounting to 2GB are copied to the target database.

However the load database process must also have to initialize the remaining 8GB of unused pages, i.e, all the individual pages must be initialized and zeroed at in case of any data that might be present in the physical region of the disk. Depending on the number of unallocated pages, the load operation takes a longer time . This is the reason why the load operation always takes a longer time than the dump operation.

The time required to perform the database dump is only dependent on the actual data(used pages) within the database. But the time required to perform a database load operation is dependent on the overall number of pages(including the used and unused pages) of the database.

Load Database command

The syntax structure of the load database command is similar in the dump database command.

```
>load database <database_name> from <dump_device_name>
```

Example:

```
>load database test from '/backup/test_full.dmp'
```

In this example the database test is restored from the dump device test_full.dmp

Restrictions: While loading the database, the users should not be connected to the target database, i.e, the target database must be in the single user mode.

The load database command must be issued from the master database.

Cross platform dumps and load

The full database dumps and load can be performed across platforms with different endian architecture. The Adaptive server automatically detects the endian architecture of the target server operating system while performing the load database and then it performs the necessary conversions. Database loads from Versions 11.9, 12.0 and 12.5 are supported.

Restrictions:

- You cannot perform cross platform transaction log dumps and load.
- Loading a password protected dump file across platform is not permitted.
- Even loading a database across platform with the database dump being prior to Version 11.9 is not supported.
- The sort order of the target server must be the same as that of the source server.

Dumping Transactions and Transaction log management

Limitations of Database Dumps:

It is not advisable to have very frequent full database dumps as they consume large amount of space and resources.

There is no way to backup modifications after the database dumps. Hence with database dumps the recovery point would be the most recent backup and you cannot perform the up to the minute recovery or point in time recovery.

Transaction log dumps

Apart from the full database dumps the Adaptive server allows for the dumping of only transaction logs.

The syntax and command structure for performing backup of the transaction logs is very much similar to that of dump database commands with the exception that password protected transaction log dumps are not allowed and you cannot load the transaction logs across platforms.

Example:

```
>dump tran(saction) <database_name> to '<file_name>'
```

```
>dump tran test to '/logbackup/test_tran1.dmp'
```

When the dump transaction command is issued,

- The adaptive server issues a checkpoint on the database.
- Copies the transaction log to a file.
- Removes the inactive portion of the log segment.(Explained in the following section)

The backing up of transaction log using dump transaction command is possible only if the database is created by separating the data segment and the log segment.

If the database is created with mixed log and data, then it is not possible to backup only the transaction log. The only option is to perform a full database backup.

The Transaction log(syslogs table)

The transaction logsegment syslogs table contains every modification made to the database. When the application or user modifies the data with the transaction statement insert, update, delete or merge, basically the modifications are recorded into the log page and then written into the data page. Both the log page and data page are processed in the data cache.

When the application or user issues a commit, the log page is immediately written to the disk(i.e, syslogs system table of the database) in order to save the modification.

Every database has its own syslogs system table which is part of logsegment.

To view the information issue:

```
>use <database_name>
```

```
>go
>sp_helpsegment 'logsegment'
```

You can view the size of the logsegment, total number of free pages available, used pages and reserved pages.

You can logically classify the contents of the syslogs table into:

- Inactive portion
- Active portion
- Unused portion

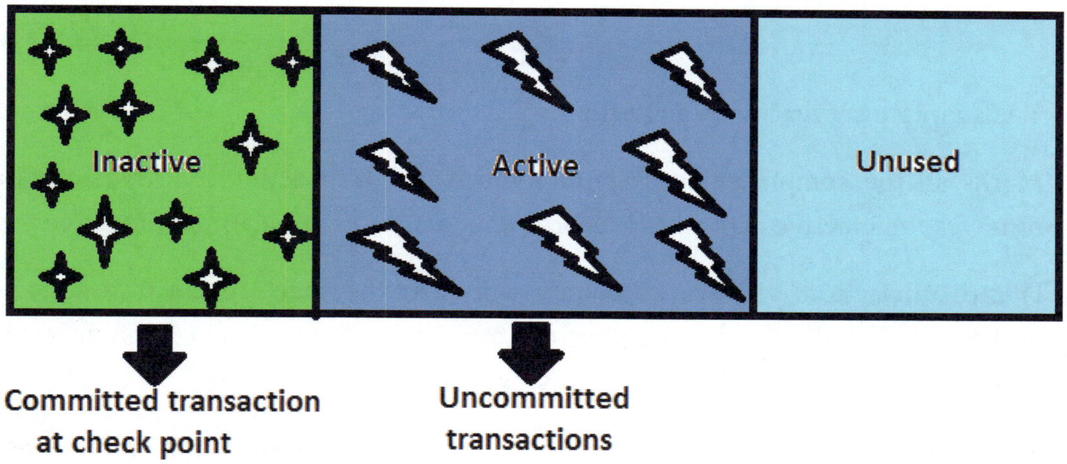

When the Adaptive server or a user issues a checkpoint on the database, the modified data page, index page and log page is written to the database and the checkpoint sequence is recorded in the logsegment syslogs table.

As the checkpoint process ensures that data is written to the database, the corresponding committed records are marked inactive in the logsegment whereas the uncommitted transactions represent the active portion.

Dump Transaction options and clearing the logsegment

As explained in earlier sections,when we use dump transaction command, the Backup server makes a copy of the transaction log and then the Adaptive server removes the inactive portion of the logsegment. This clears up space in the logsegment for further growth. In a production environment this should be the only way to clear the transaction log and reclaim space.

Other Dump transaction options

In order to clear the transaction log space we can use different options of dump transaction command.

1) With truncate_only

Example:

```
>dump transaction <database_name> with truncate_only
```

The adaptive server issues a checkpoint.

Marks all the committed transactions within the transaction log as inactive and removes the inactive committed records and records de-allocation of inactive pages.

Dump transaction with truncate_only will clear the space in the transaction log without making the backup copy of the transaction log. As such, backup server is not required to use with truncate_only option.

With truncate_only is not a good option to perform in a production database as the transaction log records will not be archived. Hence it will break the normal dump transaction sequence used with the backup server and further log dumps and invalidated.

Therefore you need to reinitiate the entire backup process by taking full database backup and transaction log backup.

However with truncate_only is a preferred option for the databases with mixed log and data and only option for clearing space is master database. This option should be used to clear the logs where the data is not important such as in test environments.

2)With no_log

Example:

```
>dump transaction <database_name> with no_log
```

This option must be used only when dump transaction with truncate_only fails.

With no_log option truncates the log without writing a checkpoint record to the log.As the command breaks the transaction log dump sequence, it is necessary to dump the database immediately after the with no_log option is used.

3)With no_truncate

Example:

```
>dump transaction <database_name> with no_truncate
```

With no_truncate option must be used with the dump transaction command whenever we are performing up to the minute recovery.

In the eventuality of media failure on the data device, the checkpoint process will not be able to write the data pages into the disk. So you need to preserve the committed records in the log device for recovery purpose.

The dump transaction with no_truncate option do not issue a checkpoint and it is used to retrieve the log from actually a failed database. It is called recovering the log. It is called recovering the log. It is a special log dump which makes a backup of the transaction log without truncating the log. Sybase manuals suggest never to use this option when the users have access to the database.

Database options :

You can truncate the transaction log when the adaptive server performs an automatic checkpoint. This is done by setting the database option "trunc log on chkpt"

Example:

```
>sp_dboption <database_name>, "trunc log on chkpt", "true"
```

This option is not suitable for production databases as you cannot make a copy of the transaction log before clearing the log.

This option is suitable for test databases where current backups are not required. Also it is suitable for databases with "mixed log and data" where you cannot perform transaction log backup.

Minimally logged Transactions

By default the databases do not allow minimally logged operations which means that every row caused by insert, update, delete and slow bcp will be recorded into the transaction log. But certain database operations need to be performed in the minimally logged mode. In the minimally logged operations, only the space allocation and de-allocation information will be recorded into the transaction log. Whereas bulk inserts, select into, fast bcp operations do not write log records into the transaction log.

Examples of minimally logged operations are copying historical data by creating a table by using source table as a template.

Example:

```
>select * into emp_copy
>from emp
```

*performing fast BCP
*write text operations
*creating a index using parallel sort
*running reorg rebuild

For the databases to allow minimally logged operations, we need to set the database option "select into/bulk copy/pll sort" "true"

Example:

```
>sp_dboption test "select into/bulk copy/plls sort", "true"
>go
```

The command must be issued from the master database.

When the database option "select into/blk copy/pll sort is true and when the user is performing a minimally logged operation, you cannot take the transaction log backup. The adaptive server breaks the log dump sequence. In this situation you need to reinitiate the backup process by performing full database backup and reinitiating the transaction log backup.

Loading Transactions

You cannot independently load a transaction log from a dump device.

The load transaction should only follow load database operation for transaction recovery.

Procedure: Restore the database using full database dump. Then apply the transaction log dumps. The transaction log dumps must be loaded in the same sequential order in which they were backed up. Note that every transaction load copies the contents into the current syslogs table and internally initiates a recovery process. So the online database command must be issued after you load the last transaction log dump. The online database command will undo all incomplete transactions.

The command structure of load transaction is similar to that of load database.

Example:

```
>load transaction <database_name> from "<file_name>"
```

Database Recovery Scenarios

Some database recovery scenarios are explained with example.

Scenario 1:Non Stop Recovery

- Database: Test
- Full database backup performed everyday at 9:30PM.
- Transaction log backup scheduled every hour.
- The logsegment are mirrored.

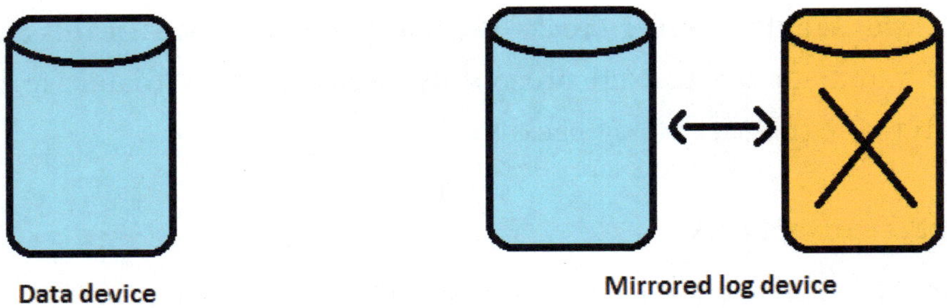

Problem: Failure of a log device reported.

Solution: The data device is intact and there is no data loss. Since the log devices are mirrored, even if one of the log devices fail, the server will continue to write in the available log device and the server automatically unmirrors the failed device and writes the message in the error log.

Replace the failed log device and run the disk remirror command. This reinitiates the log device by copying the contents of the log device to the new device and subsequent writes will happen on both the devices.

Conclusion: No need to perform database recovery and no downtime involved. It is called as non-stop recovery.

Scenario 2: Incomplete Recovery

- Database: Test
- Full database backup performed every day at 9:30PM.
- Transaction log backup scheduled for every one hour.
- The log device is not mirrored.

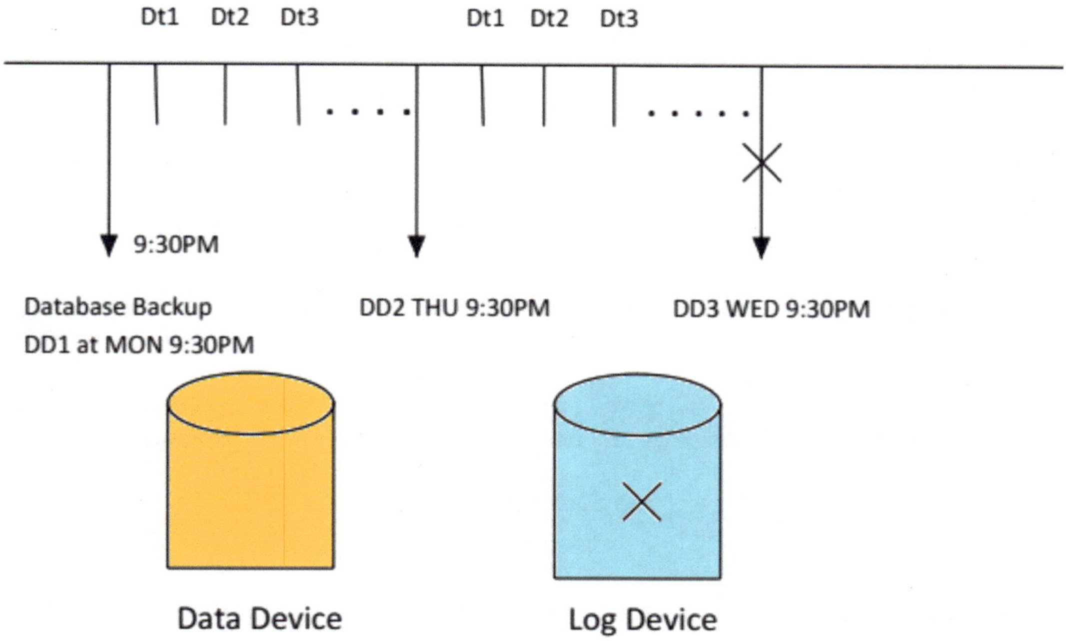

Problem: Failure of a log device reported on Wednesday at 9:15PM.

Solution: Even though the data device is intact, the database is unusable since logsegment device is corrupted and it is unmirrored. You cannot further run dump database command since the database is unusable and also you cannot run du mp transaction with no_truncate.

1) Drop the databse

If the server does not allow you to drop the database as it is damaged, you need to manually update the sysdatabases system table and change the status to 320. If the status column holds a value 320, the corresponding database is marked as suspect.

By default the system tables are not updatable. In order to update the system tables the configuration "allow updates to system table" must be changed

```
>sp_configure "allow updates to system tables", 1
>go
```

Then change the "status" column

```
>begin tran
>update sysdatabases
```

```
>set status = 320
>where name='test'
>go
>commit tran
```

Reset the configuration parameter "allow updates to system tables" back to default

```
>sp_configure "allow updates to system tables", 0
>go
```

Drop the corrupt database using dbcc dbrepair command

```
>dbcc dbrepair (test,dropdb)
>go
```

2) Create the database test with the same size as that of the dropped database by separating the data and log.

3) Load the database from the most recent full database backup, i.e, from the database dump in the 9:30PM.

4) Then apply the transactions logs up to 9:00PM.

Conclusion: You can recover the database and transactions up to Wednesday 9:00PM, i.e, up to the last valid transaction log backup. Any modifications between 9:00PM to the point of failure will be lost.

It is a case of incomplete recovery.

Scenario 3 : Upto the Minute recovery

Upto the Minute Recovery

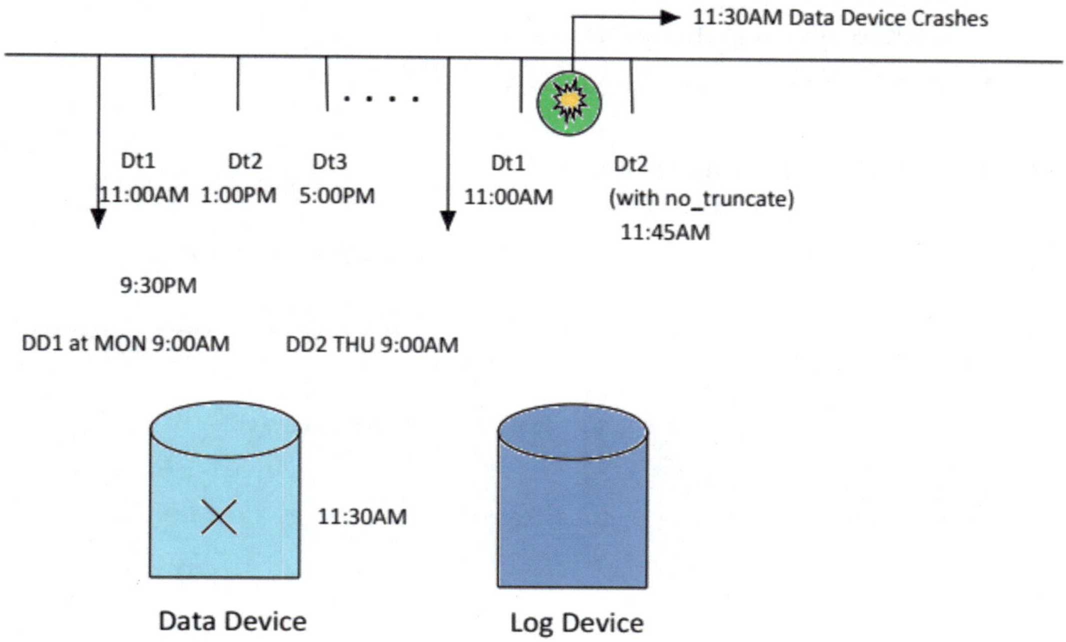

Database: Test

Full database backup is performed every day in the morning at 9:00PM before the start of the business hours. In between the full database backups, the transaction log backups are performed.

Problem: Failure of the data device is reported at 11:30AM on Tuesday.

Solution: The database is unusable since the database data device is corrupted. But the log device is intact. You cannot run the dump database after 11:30AM. Also you cannot run the dump transaction command even though the log device is intact. This is because the normal dump transaction command issues a checkpoint and the checkpoint fails as the data device is unavailable.

- Perform a special transaction log dump at 11:45AM to retrieve he log.

```
>dumptransactiontestwith no_truncate
to "/backup/test_no_trunc_trn.dmp"
```

- Drop and recreate the database.

- Load the database from the most recent backup (DD2, Tuesday 9:00AM)
- Load the transaction from the transaction log dumps since the most recent backup including the special log dump.
- Issue online database test.

Scenario 4: Point in time recovery

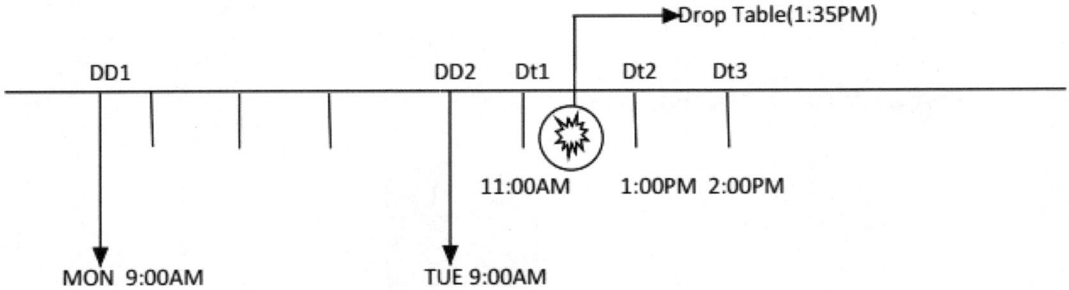

Database: Test

Full database backup is performed every day in the morning at 9:00AM before the business hours. Regularly transaction log backups are performed between the full database backups.

Problem: A user accidentally dropped a table in the test database. Need to recover the object level data.

Solution: Dropping a table is not a logical or syntactical error and the event goes unrecorded. So you need to do point-in-time recovery which is a load transaction option which allows you to partially recover a database. You can roll forward the database transactions to a particular time in the transaction log.

It is not possible to perform point-in-time recovery for the databases created with mixed log and data.

The database dump and transaction log dumps must be intact. If there are damaged by dumps prior to the time of recovering the table, then point-in-time recovery cannot be performed.

Dump the transaction log for the test database.

```
>dump transaction test to '/backup/test_tran_200pm.dmp'
```

- Load the test database from the most recent dump, (DD2, Tuesday 9:00AM)
- Load the transaction from log dumps Dt1, Dt2. This restores data modifications up to 1:00PM.
- Now load the transaction log that recorded the table drop, using the until-time option just before the table drop time.

```
>load transaction test from '/backup/test_tran_200pm.dmp

'
```

- Online the database.
- Perform full database dump and reinitiate transaction log backups.

Recovering the master database

. If the master database is corrupted due to media failures with the master device or due to any internal problems, the adaptive server cannot start. It is a downtime and you need to rebuild the master device.

In order to recover the master database as efficiently as possible, follow these recommendations.

Do not build application databases or any other databases on the master device.

Always perform the up to date backup of master device after making any changes which affects the system tables in master, such as:

- Creating and dropping databases.
- Resizing the databases with alter database.
- Initializing and resizing the devices.
- Mirroring and permanently unmirroring the device.
- Adding or dropping logins and roles.

Apart from performing the regular backup of master database, it is advised to take backup of six important system tables of the master database and also maintain the hard copy of important system tables. They are

- sysdatabases
- sysdevices

- syslogins
- sysusages
- syssrvroles
- sysloginroles

The recovery process rebuilds the master device to its default size or to a specified size, then rebuilds the master database to its default state wherein only master model, tempdb and sybsystem system databases are created on the master device.

The master database rebuild process do not rebuild the sybsystemprocs database and sysprocsdev is not initialized. So you will not be able to use the system stored procedures.

Once the master database has been rebuilt, restore the master database with the most recent master database backup.

Step by step Procedure for Rebuilding the Master database

1. If the master device area appears to be corrupt, shut down the adaptive server.

```
>shutdown
>go
```

2. Using the dataserver utility build a new master database master device and master database.

```
$ dataserver -d /sybase/data/master.dat -b60M -z2k
```

The dataserver utility creates a new master device of size 60MB and initializes the master device with 2K pages and master database is created with the default size of 13MB. The server is automatically shut down.

3. Restart the adaptive server in the single user mode. If you have chosen a different file name or path for the master device, then edit the RUN_<server_name> script and change the physical path of the master device and then restart the Adaptive server in the single user mode using the startserver utility.

```
$ startserver -f RUN_<server_name> -m
```

4. When the master database is rebuilt, the server holds a null password for the 'sa' login.

Connect to the Adaptive server.

The master database is built with the default size of 13MB. If required alter the master database to its original size

You could observe that the recovery process builds master, model, tempdb and sybsystemdb databases on the master device. Since sybsystemprocs database is not created, you cannot use any system stored procedures.

To list the databases use

```
>select name form sysdatabases
>go
```

5. Now you need to recover the master database from the most recent backup. In order to list the backup server in the sysservers system table of the master database, update the sysservers system table to make correct entry for the backup server.

```
>update sysservers
>set srvnetname = '<BACKUP_server_name>'
>where srvname= 'SYB_BACKUP>
>go
```

6. Now load the master database from the most recent backup.

```
>load database master from
from '<file_name>'
```

Once the master database is restored, the server automatically shuts down.

7. Restart the adaptive server in the normal (multiuser) mode.

```
$ startserver -f RUN_<server_name>
```

Using the original password for sa, connect to the adaptive server and check for all the databases, devices, logins appear to be restored correctly.

Disk reinit and Disk refit.

If the most recent master database backup itself is corrupted or if the master database backup is not up to date, then we need to recover all the existing devices and databases using disk reinit command.

After the most recent backup of master database, if you have created new devices and databases, the master database recovery procedure will not be able to reinitialize the new devices and databases as they will not be listed in the sysdevices, sysdatabases and sysusages system tables.

Then use disk reinit command to recover devices which are not listed in the sysdevices system table. The disk reinit command restores the information in the sysdevices system table without reinitializing the device.

Accurate values must be supplied to the disk reinit using the backup copy of the sysdevices system table.

Example:

```
>disk reinit
>name="logical_device_name"
>physname="physical path"
>vdevno=virtual_device_number
>size="<in K, M, G>"
```

Disk reinit command should be run against each new device by supplying correct values for the device name, physical path and virtual device number. Otherwise you may permanently corrupt your database.

Then run the disk refit command. The disk refit is used to rebuild the sysusages and sysdatabases system table in the master from the database fragments listed in the sysdevices system table.

Enable the traceflag 3608 and run:

```
>disk refit
>dbcc traceon (3608)
>go
>disk refit
>go
```

Once disk refit command is executed the adaptive server automatically shuts down. Restart the server in the single user mode and verify that all the databases are being restored with the correct size.

Run the dbcc commands to ensure database consistency and shut down the server.

Restart the adaptive server in the normal multiuser mode so that users can access the database.

CHAPTER – 9

MONITORING THE FREE SPACE AND SYSTEM MONITORING

OVERVIEW

Apart from initializing and creating devices and databases, the system administrators have to develop resource allocation plan, automate space usage monitoring by setting up free space and last chance thresholds. Keeping the server in a healthy order is supplemented by regularly monitoring the error logs, monitoring user processes, capturing performance statistics on a regular basis.

Managing long running transactions

Usually when the transaction log is full, we tend to clear the log space by taking transaction log backup or by using dump transaction with truncate_only. The server truncates the inactive portion of the log. The inactive part of the log is nothing but the committed transaction at the checkpoint time. This clears the log and releases the space in the logsegment.

However, sometimes frequent log backups will not clear the log space.

The uncommitted transaction records are viewed as active part of the logsegment. If the transactions are not committed for a longer duration of time, then there will be very less space to clear the logs. We can view the oldest active transactions from the syslogshold table.

The syslogshold table

The syslogshold table is part of the master database and the contents of syslogshold table are dynamically created when it is queried. When queried, the syslogshold table may be empty or it may have one row for a database representing the oldest active transaction for that database.

You can get the snapshot of the current situation for a database by querying the syslogshold table.

Example: Issue the following query to get the server process ID (spid) for the oldest active transaction.

```
>select spid, dbid, name, starttime
>form syslogshold
>where dbid = db_id('test')
```

You can further query both syslogshold and sysprocesses system tables to get the hostname and application responsible for the long running transaction.

```
>select a.program_name, a.hostname,
>b.name, b.starttime
>from sysprocesses a, syslogshold b
>where a.spid= b.spid
>and
>b.spid! = 0
```

Using the above information you may notify the end user or kill the long running transaction.

System procedures to Monitor space

sp_helpdb: Basically provides information about the relation between the devices and segments in a database. Execute the system procedure sp_helpdb within the database to view the segment data.

Example:

```
>use
>test
```

```
>go
>sp_helpdb test

Name                db_size          owner dbid
         created
                                     status

      -------- -------------------------- ----- ------
            ------------------------------------
            ------------------------------------

test                3.0 MB           sa               5
         Feb 20, 2014
         mixed log and data

(1 row affected)
device_fragments
         size               usage
         created
         free kbytes

   ------------------------------------------------------------
 -------------------------- -------------------------------------
                                         ---
       --------------------------------------------------
              --------------------------------

master
                    3.0 MB           data and log
         Feb 20 2014 12:09PM
                              1292

device              segment
------------ --------------------
master              default
master              logsegment
master              system
```

```
(return status = 0)
```

You get the information about the total size of the database, size of the data segment, size of the logsegment and segment mapping to the devices.

sp_helpsegment: Lists all the segments of a database or when used with an argument provides information about a particular segment.

Use sp_helpsegment to monitor the total pages, number of free pages left in the database.

Example:

```
>sp_helpsegment

segment  name                 status
------- -------------------- ------
        0 system             0
        1 default            1
        2 logsegment         0

(return status = 0)

>sp_helpsegment "default"

segment           name        status
------- -------------------- --------
        1 default 1

device   size                free_pages

------------ ---------- ------------

master   3.0MB               646

Objects on segment 'default':

table_name                   index_name                    indid
                   partition_name
      ------------------------------ ------------------------------
------ ------
      -------------------------------------------

syscomments                  syscomments
```

```
0
         syscomments_6
syscomments                   csyscomments
2
         csyscomments_6
sysreferences                 sysreferences
0
         sysreferences_16
sysreferences                 ncsysreferences
2
         ncsysreferences_16
sysreferences                 nc2sysreferences
3
         nc2sysreferences_16
sysreferences                 csysreferences
4
         csysreferences_16
sysusermessages               csysusermessages
1
         csysusermessages_15
sysusermessages               ncsysusermessages
2
         ncsysusermessages_15
test_tab          test_tab
0

         test_tab_576002052
test_tab          skip_ncindex
2
         skip_ncindex_576002052
Objects currently bound to segment 'default':
table_name                    index_name                    indid
------------------------------ ---------------------------------
- ------
syscomments                   syscomments
0
syscomments                   csyscomments
2
sysreferences                 sysreferences
```

```
0
sysreferences                  ncsysreferences
2
sysreferences                  nc2sysreferences
3
sysreferences                   csysreferences
4
sysusermessages                csysusermessages
1
sysusermessages                ncsysusermessages
2
test_tab          test_tab
0
test_tab ski      p_ncindex
2
total_size                              total_pages
         free_pages                     used_pages
         reserved_pages
      ---------------------------------- ------------------------
------
      ------------------------------ ------------------------------
--
      ------------------------------
3.0MB                      1536
         646               890
         0
(return status = 0)
```

The number of free page in the default segment is 646 pages.

If the number of free pages approaches zero, then you have to expand the database to add space to the data segment.

Frequently use sp_helpsegment 'logsegment' within the database to check the free space available for the logsegment.

sp_spaceused: When used without an argument, provides the amount of space used in a database. We can use the table name or index as the argument and get the information about the space used by the objects.

By periodically running sp_spaceused, you can monitor the space available in the database. Issue sp_spaceused syslogs regularly to check the size of the log.

Last chance Threshold

The last chance threshold is an estimate of the number of free pages needed to backup the transaction log and then truncate the log. The last chance threshold is automatically created for logsegment of every database. By default the last chance threshold is associated with a procedure called sp_thresholdaction and the procedure is added with the systhresholds system table.

The following diagram represents a logsegment with a last chance threshold.

Image

As the transactions cause the adaptive server to write modifications into the transaction log, the used space in the logsegment increases and the available free space reduces.

As the free space falls below the threshold value, the adaptive server executes the procedure sp_thresholdaction. However by default only the name of the procedure sp_thresholdaction is entered in the systhresholds system table, but there is no procedure sp_thresholdaction created in the database. So message is logged in the error log saying sp_thresholdaction not found and no action taken.

sp_thresholdaction

As discussed, there is no default sp_thresholdaction procedure created in the database. You need to create and customize the procedure. The procedure may contain any command such as dump transaction, dump transaction with truncate_only or database expansion commands such as alter database. Here is a sample threshold procedure which writes a message to the server's error log and performs transaction log dump.

```
>use test
   >go
   Create proc sp_thresholdaction
   (@dbname varchar(40),
```

```
@segmentname varchar(40),
@free_space int,
@status int)
as
declare @dump_name varchar(30)
select @dump_name=
@dbname + convert (varchar(60), getdate( ), 108)
dump transaction @dbname to @dump_name
print "TRANSACTION LOG DUMP:
The logsegment of %1! database is dumped",
@dbname
print "The dump file name is %1!",
@dump_name
>go
```

The adaptive server passes four parameters @dbname, @segmentname, @space_left, @status to the threshold procedure and these parameters are passed by the position and therefore they must be declared in the same order.

The print message is included in the procedure to send the dump transaction message and the dump file name to the error log. Otherwise the threshold event will not be recorded in the error log.

As the last chance threshold procedure sp_thresholdaction is added in the systhreshold system table, you need not have to explicitly add the threshold procedure using sp_addthreshold.

Once the free space in the logsegment falls below the threshold value, the adaptive server executes the system procedure sp_thresholdaction. As the sp_thresholdaction procedure includes a dump transaction command, the adaptive server performs a transaction log dump to the specified device and records a message in the error log.

Free Space Threshold

Apart from the last chance threshold on the log segment, we can create free space thresholds on any other segment. By default, no free space thresholds are set on any segment. To view the associated thresholds, issue:

```
>sp_helpthreshold
     >go
```

In addition, we can create more than one free space threshold on a given segment.

You can use free space thresholds to send notification when the space in the segment reaches a threshold level. Also you can use multiple thresholds to provide multiple warning messages. The following example illustrates using a free space threshold procedure for monitoring space in the default segment.

Example:

- Create a stored procedure to print a warning message into the error log.

```
create proc normal_alert
(@dbname varchar(30),
@segmentname varchar(30),
@space_left int,
@status int)
as
print "The number of pages in the
%1! of the %2! database is
less than %3! free pages.",
@segmentname, @dbname, @space_left
return
go
```

- The threshold procedure should be added in the systhresholds system table. Use the system procedure sp_addthreshold.

```
>sp_addthreshold database_name, segment_name,
>free space, proc_name

>sp_addthreshold test, "default", 160, normal_alert
>go
```

The procedure normal alert will be listed in the systhresholds system table.

As the number of free pages falls below 160 pages, the adaptive server executes the procedure normal_alert and a notification message is written in the error log.

To modify a threshold, use the system procedure sp_modifythreshold.

Example:

```
>sp_modifythreshold test, "default", 160,
>normal_alert, 280
```

Now the threshold procedure will be executed when the free space falls below 280 pages.

To drop a threshold procedure use sp_dropthreshold system proedure.

```
>sp_dropthreshold test, "default", 280
>go
```

Database option for Thresholds

If the database option "no free space acctg" is set to "true", then all the active free space thresholds on the data segments will be made inactive. Only the thresholds on the log segment will be active. By disabling the free space accounting the Adaptive server speeds up the recovery time. However, by disabling the free space accounting, the system procedures cannot give accurate information about space allocation.

System Monitoring

The Adaptive server needs to be constantly monitored and there must also be a preventive maintenance plan in order to maintain the Adaptive server in a good working condition. Some of the monitoring and maintenance tasks take place at the server level and they are explained in the following sections.

Adaptive Server Error log

The Adaptive server error log is created when you build the server and it islocated in the path

```
$SYBASE/$SYBASE_ASE/install
```

The file name of the error log is

```
<server_name>.log
```

The error log is a test file containing error messages. The messages are appended to the error log every time the Adaptive server is restarted. Apart from the boottime messages, the system records only major errors and anomalies of the server.

Error log format

Here is an example for error log format:

00:0112:00000:00001:2013/10/28 14:25:00:58 server

This information can be generalized as:

instance_id:thread_id:family_id:spid date timeserver/kernel message

Instance id – The first two digits represent the instance number in a clustered environment. In the case of a non-clustered environment, its value is always zero.(00)

Thread id – The thread_id appears as a four digit number. For example, if the thread_id is 0112, it indicates that the error message is from engine number 01 and the associated thread number is 12. Basically it is a combination of the engine and the associated thread on which the error has occured.

Family id – It is a five digit number indicating family_id of the originating thread. Its value is always 00000 in the case of serial processing.

In parallel processing, you could see the server process ID of the part of the originating thread.

Spid – It is a five digit number. It represents the server process ID of the thread which generated error message. For all the system tasks its value is 00000

Date – year/month/day on which the error message is written into the error log file. It is helpful in sorting the error messages by date.

Time - Time at which the error message is written. It is represented as 24_hour format.

Server/kernel – Type of the error message

Error messages:

An error message is a message which is either sent to the user or/and to the error log.

The system error messages are stored in sysmessages system table of the master database. Most of the error messages are sent to the user sessions.

Only the stack trace from the fatal error messages with severity level 19 and above are written into the error log file.

Severity levels

The severity level represents the type and severity of the problem.

The severity level error messages from 10 to 16 are generated due to the errors caused by the users and they are displayed to the user screen itself. They do not terminate the user sessions and the problems caused can be corrected by the users.

The severity level 17 error message will be reported to the user and it is due to the lack of available resources. For example, you are trying to open many parallel sessions, whereas the number of connections is restricted by the system administrator to 500.

The severity level 18 error message represents a non-fatal internal software bug. However, it does not interrupt the connections.

The severity level 19 to 26 are fatal errors which interrupt the user connections to the Adaptive server and some of the errors even shutdown the Adaptive server.

For more information about the severity level error messages refer sybase documents and reference manuals.

What to look out for?

- Within the error log you can monitor for the valid startup of you Adaptive server. Any errors reported during the Adaptive server startup may be an indication of hardware errors and it may prevent the database from coming online.

- Look out for corrupted block errors and deadlock events. All the deadlock events are recorded in the error log.
- Monitor the error log for database threshold errors. The Adaptive server sends the notification information about crossing the threshold and customized output of any print messages from the threshold procedure.

Error log sample output

00:0000:00000:00000:2014/02/08 12:39:40.94 kernel Internal run-time model set for Linux - Native

00:0000:00000:00000:2014/02/08 12:39:40.94 kernel Adaptive Server is using the threaded kernel mode.

00:0000:00000:00000:2014/02/08 12:39:40.94 kernel Using 4096 file descriptors.

00:0000:00000:00000:2014/02/08 12:39:40.94 kernel Adaptive Server Enterprise/15.7.0/EBF 19495 SMP /P/x86_64/Enterprise Linux/ase157/2820/64-bit/FBO/Fri Sep 16 00:54:35 2011

00:0000:00000:00000:2014/02/08 12:39:40.94 kernel Confidential property of Sybase, Inc.

00:0000:00000:00000:2014/02/08 12:39:40.94 kernel Copyright 1987, 2011

00:0000:00000:00000:2014/02/08 12:39:40.94 kernel Sybase, Inc. All rights reserved.

Managing the error log

The Adaptive server appends the server startup message to the error log and the error log starts and stops with the Adaptive server. Over a period of time, the error log may grow quite large enough to fill the file system. If there is not enough space for the error log to grow, then the Adaptive server may stop functioning. As a maintenance task, periodically move the error log to another location during server restarts.

PROCESS MONITORING

Any task executed by the Adaptive server is called a process. The process can be initiated by a user and by the Adaptive server. Each process is uniquely identified by a number called server process id, "spid".

All the information related to a process is stored in the sysprocesses system table in the master database. A process can also belong to a "family of processes", wherein it is given a family ID, identified as "fid"

Run the system procedure sp_who to list the information about the current running process.

```
    >sp_who
>go
Fid        spid     status                           loginame orignname
           Hostname                                  blk_spid dbname
           Cmd                                       block_xloid
      ------ ------ ----------------------- -------- --------
      ------------------------------------------ -------- -------
-----
      -------------------------------------- -----------
   0       2 sleeping                                NULL     NULL
   NULL                                                       0 master
   DEADLOCK TUNE                                              0
   0       3 sleeping                                NULL     NULL
   NULL                                                       0 master
   ASTC HANDLER                                               0
   0       4 sleeping                                NULL     NULL
   NULL                                                       0 master
   CHECKPOINT SLEEP                                           0
   0       5 sleeping                                NULL     NULL
   NULL                                                       0 master
   HK WASH                                                    0
   0       6 sleeping                                NULL     NULL
   NULL                                                       0 master
   HK GC                                                      0
   0       7 sleeping                                NULL     NULL
   NULL                                                       0 master
```

```
HK CHORES                                               0
0      8 sleeping                          NULL     NULL
NULL                                                    0 master
PORT MANAGER                                            0
0      9 sleeping                          NULL     NULL
NULL                                                    0 master
NETWORK HANDLER                                         0
0      10 sleeping                         NULL     NULL
NULL                                                    0 master
LICENSE HEARTBEAT                                       0
0      12 running               sa                  sa
localhost.localdomain                                   0 test
INSERT                                                  0

(10 rows affected)
(return status = 0)
```

The Adaptive server processes can be classified into three types, namely:

System processes – They are initiated by the Adaptive server and show a login name NULL, running at the database master. They always show a status "sleeping". Example of system processes are DEADLOCK TUNE, ASTC HANDLER, HK WASH, etc.

Worker processes – Worker processes are invoked during parallel processing.

User process – Invoked by the user session.

The process status can be any of the following:

runnable: A task waiting in the queue
running: currently executing process
sleeping: waiting for the system resources such as disk I/O
Recv sleep: waiting on a network send
lock sleep: The process waiting to acquire a lock
log suspend: The process suspended by the Adaptive server for crossing the last chance threshold.
Background: a background task run by the Adaptive server such as a threshold process.

Killing a process

A process can be killed by the system administrator. The most common reason to kill a process is because it is contending with other users.

The process may be holding locks and/or blocking system resources.

The server will allow you to kill a process only if it is able to rollback the transactions and clean up all the system resources.

Syntax: kill spid

Example:

```
>kill 369
>go
```

Restrictions -

- You cannot kill your own process.
- A kill command cannot be used within a transaction.
- The system processes cannot be killed.
- A system administrator can kill process with the status such as "running" or "runnable", any process with network send or receive, log suspend, waiting for a lock, alarm sleep, etc.

sp_lock

The Adaptive server should be periodically monitored for lock contention using the system procedure sp_lock.

sp_lock provides information about the process currently holding locks. The lock contention occurs when multiple users try to access the same data structures which are already locked by a user.

The sp_lock procedure when used without an argument may produce a lengthy output. Generally sp_lock system procedure is used in conjunction with sp_who.

First use the sp_who procedure to identify the process which are causing lock contention. Then, using the spid as a argument with sp_lock procedure you can derive more information such as the table_id, lock types held by the process.

Example:

```
>sp_lock spid
>go
```

sp_object_stats

The sp_object_stats system procedure provides lock statistics information for tables and indexes. You can filter the output for top N tables. To list the top 20 tables which report high lock contention over a period of 10 minutes, issue:

```
>sp_object_stats "00:10", 20
     >go
```

Activity performance monitoring

The adaptive server comes with various system procedures and tools to dynamically monitor the activity on the server. Utilize these tools to monitor the server performance on a regular basis by scheduling jobs and also non-periodically at the server peak activity.

sp_monitor

You can use the sp_monitor system procedure for tracking CPU usage, number of physical I/Os performed by a statement. Just to report how busy your Adaptive server is, use:

```
>sp_monitor
     >go
```

sp_monitorcontig

You can use the system procedure sp_monitorconfig to keep track of the memory utilization of many system parameters. The sp_monitorconfig provides information about cache memory usage statistics related to metadata descriptors used by the database, objects and indexes.

Example:

```
>sp_monitorconfig "<configuration_name>"
    >go
>sp_monitorconfig "number of user connections"
    >go
```

```
Usage information at date and time: Feb 20 2014 2:28PM.

Name                                                  Num_free

Num_active

        Pct_act          Max_Used          Num_Reuse

    -------------------------------------------------- --------
--- -----------
             ------------ ----------- -----------

number of user connection                             24

1

        4.00             1                 0
(return status = 0)
```

```
>sp_monitorconfig "procedure cache size"
```

```
Usage information at date and time: Feb 20 2014 2:28PM.

Name                                                  Num_free

Num_active

        Pct_act          Max_Used          Num_Reuse

    -------------------------------------------------- --------
--- -----------
             ------------ ----------- -----------

procedure cache size                                  5722

1278

        18.26            1567              0
(return status = 0)
```

```
>sp_monitorconfig "all"
```

```
Usage information at date and time: Feb 20 2014 2:30PM.

Name                                                      Num_free

Num_active

         Pct_act            Max_Used             Num_Reuse

      ------------------------------------------------------ -----------
--- -----------
                ------------ ----------- -----------

additional network memory                                  559212
561584
         50.11              561584               0
audit queue size                                           100
0
         0.00               0                    0
disk i/o structures                                        256
0
         0.00               239                  0
heap memory per user                                       4096
0
         0.00               0                    0
max cis remote connection                                  100
0
         0.00               0                    0
max memory                                                 12493
28467
         69.50              28467                0
max number network listen                                  4
1
         20.00              1                    0
max online engines                                         0
1
         100.00             1                    0
memory per worker process                                  512 512
         50.00              512                  0
number of alarms                                           28 12
         30.00              12                   0
number of aux scan descri                                  256
0
```

```
        0.00             0                  0
number of devices                                   7
3
        30.00            3                  0
number of dtx participant                           500 0
        0.00             0                  0
number of java sockets                              42 0
        0.00             0                  0
number of large i/o buffe                           6 0
        0.00             1                  0
number of locks                                     4914
86
        1.72             118                0
number of mailboxes                                 29
1
        3.33             1                  0
number of messages                                  64
0
        0.00             0                  0
number of open databases                            5 7
        58.33            7                  0
number of open indexes                              472
28
        5.60             29                 0
number of open objects                              465
35
        7.00             36                 0
number of open partitions                           472
28
        5.60             29                 0
number of remote connection                         20
0
        0.00             0                  0
number of remote logins                             20
0
        0.00             0                  0
number of remote sites                              10
0
        0.00             0                  0
```

```
number of sort buffers                                        500
0
         0.00                48                 0
number of user connection                                     24
1
         4.00                1                  0
number of worker processes                                    1
0
         0.00                0                  0
partition groups                                              1024
0
         0.00                0                  0
permission cache entries                                      15
0
         0.00                0                  0
procedure cache size                                          5721
1279
         18.27               1567               0
size of global fixed heap                                     150
0
         0.00                0                  0
size of process object he                                     1500
0
         0.00                0                  0
size of shared class heap                                     1536
0
         0.00                0                  0
size of unilib cache                                          264202
592
0.22 592 0
txn to pss ratio                                              400
0
         0.00                0                  0
(return status = 0)
```

sp_sysmon

There are many third party and sybase utilities used for system monitoring.Perhaps sp_sysmon is the most comprehensive one and no other tool can give you the detailed information as provided by sp_sysmon.

The sp_sysmon system procedure provides a snapshot of complete server activity for a given interval of time. This data is very useful for identifying and analyzing the bottlenecks during periods of intensive server usage.

Run the sp_sysmon:

- Before or after a performance tuning activity
- When slowish server performance is reported.

The sp_sysmon contributes to server overhead. The amount overhead increases with more CPUs.

Example:

```
>sp_sysmon "00:00:40"
```

provides a dynamic snapshot report of the server status over a sampling period of 40 seconds.

```
==========================================================================
===============
   Sybase Adaptive Server Enterprise System Performance Report
==========================================================================
===============

Server Version:        Adaptive Server Enterprise/15.7.0/EBF
                       19495 SMP /P/x86_64/Enterprise
                       Linux/ase157/2820/64-bit/FBO/Fri Sep 16
                       00:
                       54:35 2011
Run Date:                  Mar 26, 2014
Sampling Started at:       Mar 26, 2014 14:37:15
Sampling Ended at:         Mar 26, 2014 14:37:55
Sample Interval:           00:00:40
Sample Mode:               No Clear
Counters Last Cleared:     Mar 24, 2014 10:23:43
Server Name:               Test
```

```
=============================================================================
===============

Kernel Utilization
------------------

Engine Utilization (Tick %) User Busy System Busy I/O Busy Idle
-------------------------  ----------  ----------  ---------- -
ThreadPool:       syb_default_pool
Engine 0                    0.2 %     0.0 %     0.2 %
99.5 %
Average Runnable            1 min     5 min     15 min %
Tasks of total
----------------------   -------    ------    --------
ThreadPool:       syb_default_pool
Global Queue                0.0       0.0       0.0
0.0 %
Engine 0                    0.0       0.6       0.8
100.0 %
------------------------- ------------ ------------ ----------
Server Summary     Total    0.0       0.6       0.8
                 Average    0.0       0.3       0.4
CPU Yields by Engine     per sec  per xact  count %
of total
------------------------- ------------ ------------ -----------
ThreadPool:       syb_default_pool
Engine 0
Full Sleeps                 29.3      106.5     1172
96.5 %
Interrupted Sleeps          1.1       3.8       42 3.5 %

Thread Utilization (OS %)   User Busy   System Busy   Idle
------------------------   -----------  -----------  ------
ThreadPool:  syb_blocking_pool :  no activity during sample

ThreadPool :  syb_default_pool
Thread 2  (Engine 0)        0.2 %     0.1 %     99.7 %

ThreadPool : syb_system_pool
Thread 1 (Signal Handler)    0.0 %     0.0 %   100.0 %

------------------------  --------  ------  ------
```

```
Pool Summary        Total     0.0 %     0.0 %     300.0 %
                  Average     0.0 %     0.0 %     100.0 %

------------------------- ------------ ------------ ----------
Server Summary      Total     0.2 %     0.1 %     799.7 %
                  Average     0.0 %     0.0 %     100.0 %

Adaptive Server threads are consuming 0.0 CPU units.
Throughput (committed xacts per CPU unit) : 84.6
```

Comprehensive description and analysis of all the sections of the sp_sysmon report is beyond the scope of this book. However, a few important sp_sysmon management reports are explained in brief.

The output from sp_sysmon can be classified into the following sections:

Kernel Utilization

It reports on all the server engines with percentage busy usage and with number of network and disk I/O checks, CPU yields to the operating system, average wait statistics for the number I/Os.

Example:

```
>sp_sysmon "00:00:30", kernel, noclear
      >go
```

```
=================================================================
===============
   Sybase Adaptive Server Enterprise System Performance Report
=================================================================
===============

Server Version:           Adaptive  Server  Enterprise/15.7.0/EBF
                          19495    SMP    /P/x86_6    4/Enterprise
                          Linux/ase157/2820/64-bit/FBO/Fri    Sep
                          16 00: 54:35 2011
Run Date:                  Mar 26, 2014
Sampling Started at:       Mar 26, 2014 14:38:01
Sampling Ended at:         Mar 26, 2014 14:38:31
Sample Interval:           00:00:30
Sample Mode:               No Clear
```

```
Counters Last Cleared:      Mar 24, 2014 10:23:42
Server Name:                Test
================================================================
===============
================================================================
===============

Kernel Utilization
------------------
Engine Utilization (Tick %) User Busy System Busy I/O Busy
Idle
------------------------- ---------- ---------- ---------- -
ThreadPool:        syb_default_pool
Engine                       0 1.0 %  0.0 %    1.0 %
98.0 %

Average Runnable Tasks      1 min     5 min     15 min %
of total
------------------------- ------------ ------------ ---------- -
---------
ThreadPool:        syb_default_pool
Global Queue                 0.0       0.0       0.0
0.0 %
Engine 0                     0.0       0.5       0.8
100.0 %

------------------------- ------------ ------------ ----------
Server Summary     Total     0.0       0.5       0.8
                   Average   0.0       0.3       0.4

CPU Yields by Engine         per sec  per xact  count %
of total
------------------------- ------------ ------------ ---------- -
---------
ThreadPool : syb_default_pool
Engine 0
Full Sleeps                  29.2      67.5      877
85.2 %
Interrupted Sleeps           5.1       11.7      152
14.8 %
```

Engine Busy Utilization: It reports the percentage of time the server is busy executing tasks on each engine. It usually differs from the CPU usage report from the operating system monitoring tool. The operating system monitoring tools may report CPU busy of 90% but still the sp_sysmon output may produce a CPU busy percentage of 20%! This is because the sp_sysmon does not include the time looking for tasks.

Application Management

This reports execution statistics for user tasks. This is particularly useful if you tune your application by assigning a task on priority base to an engine. You can obtain information related to the tasks which are switching between different priority levels, whether low priority tasks are getting starved for CPU time.

Example:

```
>sp_sysmon "00:00:30", @applmon = appl_and_login
>go
```

```
===============================================================================
Sybase Adaptive Server Enterprise System Performance Report
===============================================================================

Server Version:           Adaptive Server Enterprise/15.7.0/EBF
                          19495     SMP     /P/x86_64/Enterprise
                          Linux/ase157/2820/64-bit/FBO/Fri   Sep
                          16 00: 54:35 2011
Run Date:                 Mar 26, 2014
Sampling Started at:      Mar 26, 2014 14:39:09
Sampling Ended at:        Mar 26, 2014 14:39:39
Sample Interval:          00:00:30
Sample Mode:              No Clear
Counters Last Cleared:    Mar 24, 2014 10:23:42
Server Name: Test
===============================================================================

Kernel Utilization
------------------
```

```
Engine Utilization (Tick %) User Busy System Busy I/O Busy
Idle
------------------------- ---------- ------------ ---------- -
---------
ThreadPool:        syb_default_pool
Engine 0                    0.3 %     0.0 %     1.0 %
98.7 %

Average Runnable Tasks      1 min     5 min     15 min %
of total
------------------------- ------------ ------------ ---------- -
---------
ThreadPool:        syb_default_pool
Global Queue                0.0       0.0       0.0
0.0 %
Engine 0                    0.0       0.4       0.8
100.0 %

------------------------- ------------ ------------ ----------
Server Summary    Total     0.0       0.4       0.8
                  Average   0.0       0.2       0.4

CPU Yields by Engine       per sec   per xact   count %
of total
------------------------- ------------ ------------ ---------- -
---------
ThreadPool : syb_default_pool
Engine 0
         Full Sleeps                 29.7       80.9       890
94.7 %
         Interrupted Sleeps          1.7        4.5        50
5.3 %

Thread Utilization (OS %)    User Busy    System    BusyIdle
------------------------- ---------- -------- ----------
ThreadPool : syb_blocking_pool : no activity during sample

ThreadPool : syb_default_pool
Thread 2          (Engine 0)         0.2 %     0.1 %     99.6 %

ThreadPool : syb_system_pool
Thread 1          (Signal Handler)   0.0 %     0.0 %     100.0 %
```

```
Thread 8              (DiskController)  0.0 %     0.0 %     100.0 %
------------------------ ------------ ------------ ----------

Pool Summary          Total             0.1 %     0.0 %     299.9 %
                      Average           0.0 %     0.0 %     100.0 %

------------------------ ------------ ------------ ----------
Server Summary        Total             0.3 %     0.1 %     799.6 %
                      Average           0.0 %     0.0       % 99.9 %
```

Data Cache Management

This provides summary information for all caches and detailed statistics for each named cache.

For example, you get information about cache utilization, cache hits and misses, cache turnover, spin lock contention.

Example:

```
>sp_sysmon "00:00:30", dcache
    >go
```

```
===============================================================
===============
   Sybase Adaptive Server Enterprise System Performance Report
===============================================================
===============
Server Version:            Adaptive  Server  Enterprise/15.7.0/EBF
                           19495     SMP     /P/x86_64/Enterprise
                           Linux/ase157/2820/64-bit/FBO/Fri   Sep
                           16 00: 54:35 2011
Run Date:                   Mar 26, 2014
Sampling Started at:        Mar 26, 2014 14:39:44
Sampling Ended at:          Mar 26, 2014 14:40:14
Sample Interval:            00:00:30
Sample Mode:                No Clear
Counters Last Cleared:      Mar 24, 2014 10:23:49
Server Name:                Test
===============================================================
===============
```

```
==========================================================================
===============

Data Cache Management
---------------------

Cache Statistics Summary (All Caches)

-------------------------------------
                  per sec          per xact          count %
of total
                  ------------     ------------      ----------
----------
Cache Search Summary
         Total Cache Hits          25956.9  194676.5 778706
96.6 %
         Total Cache Misses        906.4    6798.3   27193
3.4 %
------------------------- ------------ ------------ ----------
         Total Cache Searches      26863.3  201474.8 805899

         Cache Turnover
         Buffers Grabbed           19485.3  146140.0 584560
n/a
         Buffers Grabbed Dirty     0.0      0.0      0
0.0 %

Cache Strategy Summary
         Cached (LRU) Buffers      20188.3  151412.5 605650
44.6 %
         Discarded (MRU) Buffers   25073.2  188049.3 752197
55.4 %

Large I/O Usage
                                   0.0      0.0      0
n/a

Large I/O Effectiveness
         Pages by Lrg I/O Cached   0.0      0.0      0
n/a
```

```
Asynchronous Prefetch Activity
         APFs Issued                18481.1  138608.5 554434
75.5 %
APFs Denied Due To
         APF I/O Overloads          0.1      0.8      3
0.0 %
         APF Limit Overloads        9.9      74.3     297
0.0 %
         APF Reused Overloads       0.2      1.5      6
0.0 %
APF Buffers Found in Cache
         With Spinlock Held         86.8     651.0    2604
0.4 %
         W/o Spinlock Held          5886.5   44148.5  176594
24.1 %
-----------------------------     --------  -------  ------
Total APFs Requested                24464.6  183484.5 733938
```

Disk I/O Management

It provides a report on disk I/O. For each logical device this report gives a summary and percentage reads, writes and semaphore contention.

Example:

```
>sp_sysmon "00:00:30", "diskio"
      >go
```

```
===============================================================
===============
Sybase Adaptive Server Enterprise System Performance Report
===============================================================
===============

Server Version:           Adaptive  Server  Enterprise/15.7.0/EBF
                          19495     SMP     /P/x86_64/Enterprise
                          Linux/ase157/2820/64-bit/FBO/Fri   Sep
                          16 00: 54:35 2011
Run Date:                  Mar 26, 2014
Sampling Started at:       Mar 26, 2014 14:40:25
Sampling Ended at:         Mar 26, 2014 14:40:55
```

```
Sample Interval:            00:00:30
Sample Mode:                No Clear
Counters Last Cleared:      Mar 24, 2014 10:23:46
Server Name:                Test
================================================================
===============
================================================================
===============

Disk I/O Management
-------------------

Max Outstanding I/Os        per sec     per xact    count %
of total
------------------------  ---------  ----------  --------
----------
         Server                          n/a         n/a        256
n/a
         Engine 0                        n/a         n/a        256
n/a

I/Os Delayed by
         Disk I/O Structures             n/a         n/a        3
n/a
         Server Config Limit             n/a         n/a        0
n/a
         Engine Config Limit             n/a         n/a        0
n/a
         Operating System Limit          n/a         n/a        0
n/a

Total Requested Disk I/Os                4977.2      74658.0  149316

Completed Disk I/O's
  Asynchronous I/O's
         Total Completed I/Os            4977.2      74658.5  149317
100.0 %
  Synchronous I/O's
         Total Completed I/Os            0.0         0.0        0
n/a
------------------------- ------------ ------------ ---------
```

```
Total Completed I/Os                4977.2   4658.5   149317

Device Activity Detail
----------------------

Device:
  /media/9a8125cd-5f78-4edb-8ed5-84197c0aee10/dat/ams_data.dat
  ams_data                   per sec    per xact    count %
of total
------------------------  ---------  ----------  --------
----------
  Reads
         APF                        038.7    60580.0  121160
93.6 %
         Non-APF                    277.9    4169.0   8338
6.4 %
         Writes                     0.0      0.0      0
0.0 %
  -------------------------  ------------  ------------  ----------
----------
Total I/Os                          4316.6   64749.0  129498
86.7 %
```

Lock Management

This provides information about locks, deadlocks, lock contention and lock promotion.

Example:

```
>sp_sysmon "00:00:30", "locks"
      >go
```

```
===================================================================
===============
   Sybase Adaptive Server Enterprise System Performance Report
===================================================================
===============
```

```
Server Version:              Adaptive  Server  Enterprise/15.7.0/EBF
                             19495     SMP      /P/x86_64/Enterprise
                             Linux/ase157/2820/64-bit/FBO/Fri    Sep
                             16 00: 54:35 2011
Run Date:                     Mar 26, 2014
Sampling Started at:          Mar 26, 2014 15:21:03
Sampling Ended at:            Mar 26, 2014 15:21:33
Sample Interval:              00:00:30
Sample Mode:                  No Clear
Counters Last Cleared:        Mar 24, 2014 10:23:42
Server Name:                  Test
===============================================================
===============
===============================================================
===============

Lock Management
---------------
Lock Summary                  per sec    per xact   count %
of total
------------------------  ---------  ----------  --------
----------
Total Lock Requests           33.0       495.0      990
n/a
Avg Lock Contention           0.0        0.0        0
0.0 %
Cluster Locks Retained        0.0        0.0        0
0.0 %
Deadlock Percentage           0.0        0.0        0
0.0 %

Lock Detail                   per sec    per xact   count %
of total
------------------------  ---------  ----------  --------
----------
Table Lock Hashtable
         Lookups                         5.3        80.0       160
n/a
         Avg Chain Length                n/a        n/a        0.06875
n/a
```

```
          Spinlock Contention            n/a       n/a       n/a
0.0 %

Exclusive Table
          Granted                        0.0       0.5       1
100.0 %
          Waited                         0.0       0.0       0
0.0 %
  ------------------------- ------------ ------------ ----------
----------
Total EX-Table Requests                  0.0       0.5       1
0.1 %

Shared Table
          Total SH-Table Requests        0.0       0.0       0
n/a

Exclusive Intent
          Total EX-Intent Requests       0.0       0.0       0
n/a

Shared Intent
          Granted                        5.3       79.5      159
100.0 %
          Waited                         0.0       0.0       0
0.0 %
------------------------- ------------ ------------ ---------- -
---------
Total SH-Intent Requests                 5.3       79.5      159
16.1 %

Page & Row Lock HashTable
          Lookups                        30.4      456.0     912
n/a
          Avg Chain Length               n/a       n/a       0.00000
n/a
          Spinlock Contention            n/a       n/a       n/a

0.0 %
```

You get the summary of total lock activity during the sampling period such as total lock requests, average lock contention, deadlock percentage, etc.

CHAPTER – 10
DATABASE CONSISTENCY CHECKS

A system administrator has to look out for data inconsistencies as and when they occur in a database. Even though the data inconsistencies are extremely rare, you cannot ignore them. A system administrator needs to find and correct them. There may be physical or logical corruptions in the data pages. The most common reasons being-

- improper data recovery
- hardware failure
- disk faults
- power fluctuations, etc

DATABASE CONSISTENCY CHECKER (DBCC)

The DBCC commands are similar to SQL commands. They are issued within the isql. Many of the DBCC commands need sa_role and/or sybase_ts_role to run.

Basically, the database consistency checker commands are used for checking the physical and logical consistency of the database.

Understanding Allocation page and Object Allocation

When a device is initialized, the device initialization process divides the space into allocation units. Each allocation unit is a group of 32 extents and each extent is a group of 8 contiguous pages.

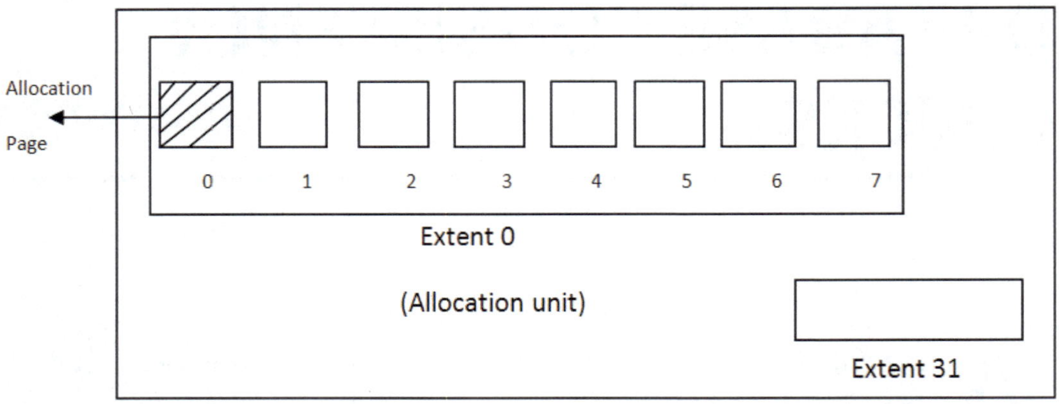

The first page of every allocation unit is called allocation page. For example, if you create a device of size 10MB for a 2K page server, the space will be uniformly divided into 20 allocation units. Each allocation unit will have one allocation page and it will be the first page of every allocation unit such as page number 0, 256, 512, 768, 1024, etc are allocation pages.

The allocation page stores information about the "space usage" by the objects within the allocation unit, i.e, when the table's data grows and when the page is full, the adaptive server allocates the next page within the extent for the table. When the table data grows and fills up an extent, the adaptive server looks for an available free extent within the allocation unit and then allocates the extent for the table which needs space.

Every time space is allocated or de-allocated, the adaptive server records the event in the allocation page.

In other words, by scanning the allocation page, you can track the allocated pages for the objects within the allocated units.

Object Allocation Map (OAM) Page

When a table is created, the adaptive server allocates a free extent for a table. The first page of the extent (belonging to a table) is called object allocation map page or OAM page.

The OAM page will have entries which points to the allocation page of an allocation unit where the table's data is stored.

For example, consider a table with the name of employee. Consider that the employee table is allocated-

Extent number 1 form allocation unit 1
Extent number 35 from allocation unit 2 and
Extent number 70 from allocation unit 3

Then as shown in figure

Page number 8 will be the OAM page and the OAM page will point to the page number 0 and page number 256 and page number 512, which are the allocation pages.

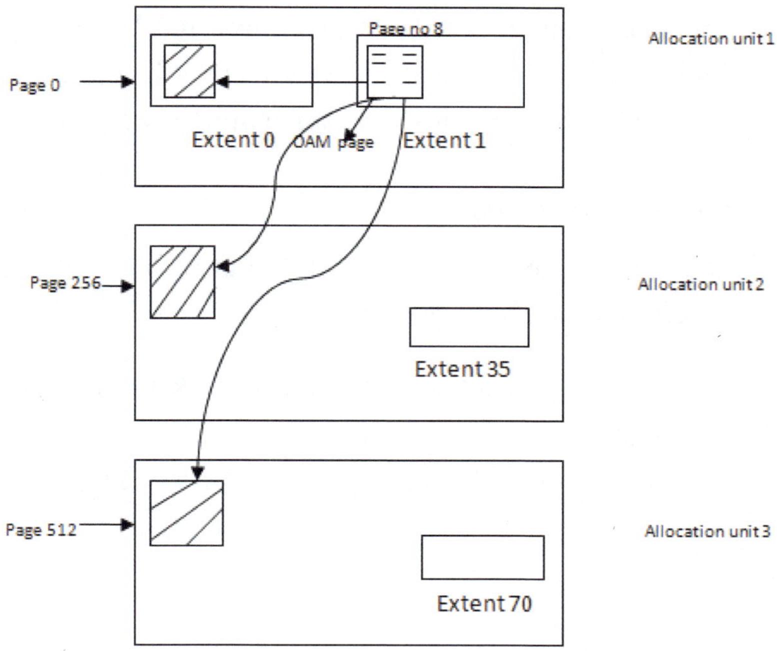

The OAM page of an object points to the allocation pages and the allocation pages in turn tracks the extents and pages.

Page Linkage

For all the APL(All Page Locking) tables, the allocated page is linked with the other pages of the object.

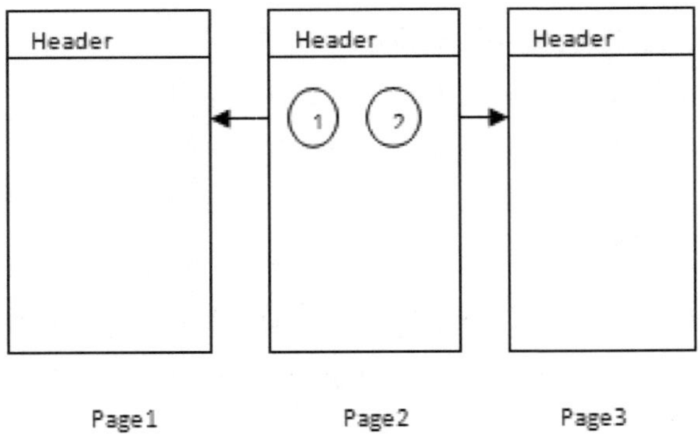

As shown in the above figure every page has a header, which stores the page number of the previous page and the next page (need not be the next immediate page). It is a doubly linked list called page linkage. Whenever a new page is allocated, the page header information of the surrounding pages will be altered.

Possible Errors or Inconsistencies

The adaptive server may record a page as allocated to a table, but in actuality the page may not be part of a page linkage chain.

- A newly allocated page may be part of a page linkage chain, but the record may be missing in the allocation page.
- There might be referential integrity problems between the system tables.

DBCC COMMANDS

The dbcc commands are utility commands which are used to check the physical and logical consistency of a database.

The page linkage information and data pointers at the page and row level are checked using:

dbcc checktable
dbcc checkdb
dbcc checkstorage

The page allocation errors are checked by

dbcc tablealloc
dbcc indexalloc
dbcc checkalloc
dbcc checkverify
dbcc checkstorage

To check the referential integrity problems within the sysetm tables, use

dbcc checkcatalog

To check the corruptions in a text or image columns, use

dbcc textalloc

RECOMMENDATIONS:

- Run the dbcc commands as part of regular maintenance
- To find the extent of damage whenever a system error has been reported
- Before backing up critical databases
- If a particular table is corrupted then run the dbcc commands to verify whether other tables of the database are corrupted
- Run the commands when the system usage is low
- For production servers, dump the database and restore it on another server and then run the dbcc commands

Examples:

```
>dbcc checkable (test_tab)
>go
```

```
Checking table 'test_tab' (object ID 1872006669): Logical page
size is 2048
bytes.
The total number of data pages in partition 'test_tab_1872006669'
(partition ID
1872006669) is 1.
The total number of data pages in this table is 1.
Table has 0 data rows.
DBCC execution completed. If DBCC printed error messages, contact
a user with
System Administrator (SA) role.
```

```
>dbcc checktable (test_tab, skip_ncindex)
>go
Checking table 'test_tab' (object ID 1872006669): Logical page
size is 2048
bytes.
The total number of data pages in partition 'test_tab_1872006669'
(partition ID
1872006669) is 1.
The total number of data pages in this table is 1.
Table has 0 data rows.
DBCC executicn completed. If DBCC printed error messages, contact
a user with
System Administrator (SA) role.
```

The command performs a consistency check by skipping the non-clustered index on a table.

To perform consistency checks on the entire database:

```
>dbcc checkdb (test)
>go


Checking test: Logical pagesize is 2048 bytes
```

```
Checking table 'sysobjects' (object ID 1): Logical page size is
2048 bytes.
The total number of data pages in partition 'sysobjects_1'
(partition ID 1) is
2.
The total number of data pages in this table is 2.
Table has 31 data rows.
Checking table 'sysindexes' (object ID 2): Logical page size is
2048 bytes.
The total number of data pages in partition 'sysindexes_2'
(partition ID 2) is
6.
The total number of data pages in this table is 6.
Table has 71 data rows.
Checking table 'syscolumns' (object ID 3): Logical page size is
2048 bytes.
The total number of data pages in partition 'syscolumns_3'
(partition ID 3) is
13.
The total number of data pages in this table is 13.
Table has 445 data rows.
Checking table 'systypes' (object ID 4): Logical page size is 2048
bytes.
The total number of data pages in partition 'systypes_4'
(partition ID 4) is 2.
The total number of data pages in this table is 2.
Table has 42 data rows.
Checking table 'syslogs' (object ID 8): Logical page size is 2048
bytes.
The total number of data pages in partition 'syslogs_8' (partition
ID 8) is 9.
The total number of data pages in this table is 9.
Table has 165 data rows.
Checking table 'syspartitions' (object ID 28): Logical page size
is 2048 bytes.
```

To perform checks on the referential integrity problems between the system tabels, use:

```
>dbcc checkcatalog
>go
```

```
Checking current database: Logical pagesize is 2048 bytes
The following segments have been defined for database 1 (database
name master).
virtual device number   virtual start addr   size (logical pages)
segments
---------------------   ------------------   ------------------
--------------------
0                  4                  6656
                                      0
                                      1
                                      2
DBCC executicn completed. If DBCC printed error messages, contact
a user with
System Administrator (SA) role.
```

In order to check page allocation errors:

```
>dbcc checkalloc
>go
```

```
Checking current database: Logical pagesize is 2048 bytes
Database 'master' is not in single user mode - may find spurious
allocation
problems due to transactions in progress.
***************************************************************
TABLE: sysobjects          OBJID = 1
PARTITION ID=1 FIRST=1 ROOT=1 SORT=0
Data level: indid 0, partition 1. 5 Data pages allocated and 1
Extents
allocated.
PARTITION ID=1 FIRST=161 ROOT=160 SORT=1
Indid : 2, partition : 1. 3 Index pages allocated and 2 Extents
allocated.
PARTITION ID=1 FIRST=10 ROOT=9 SORT=0
Indid : 3, partition : 1. 2 Index pages allocated and 1 Extents
allocated.
TOTAL # of extents = 4
***************************************************************
TABLE: sysindexes          OBJID = 2
```

```
PARTITION ID=2 FIRST=16 ROOT=16 SORT=0
Data level: indid 0, partition 2. 12 Data pages allocated and 2
Extents

      >dbcc tablealloc (test_tab)
      >go

The default report option of OPTIMIZED is used for this run.
The default fix option of FIX is used for this run.
***************************************************************
TABLE: test_tab              OBJID = 1872006669
PARTITION ID=1872006669 FIRST=3081 ROOT=3081 SORT=0
Data level: indid 0, partition 1872006669. 1 Data pages allocated
and 1 Extents
allocated.
TOTAL # of extents = 1
Alloc page 3072 (# of extent=1 used pages=2 ref pages=2)
Total (# of extent=1 used pages=2 ref pages=2) in this database
DBCC execution completed. If DBCC printed error messages, contact
a user with
System Administrator (SA) role.
```

The output of all these dbcc commands contains the information about:

- The list of objects that are being checked.
- Error messages related to the problems detected by the dbcc.

DBCC Checkstorage and Configuring dbccdb Database

Some minor drawbacks of running the above mentioned dbcc commands are:

- They lock tables or pages for extended period of time.
- The speed of checktable, checkdb, tablealloc,indexalloc with full option are slow and consume resources.
- Cannot store as historical data for deferred analysis.
- The dbcc checkstorage command is a special command which encompasses all the dbcc commands in a simple command, "dbcc checkstorage"

Advantages of dbcc Checkstorage

- The dbcc checkstorage combines the functionality of dbcc checktable, dbcc checkdb, dbcc checkalloc, dbcc tablealloc, dbccindexalloc
- Uses additional worker processes during the check storage operation and hence parallel execution is achieved.
- The command uses a separate database called "dbccdb" to store the results of the checks made on the target database.
- Storing information as historical data in dbccdb database allows for trend analysis and by using system stored procedure, you can generate reports.
- The speed of checking is very fast without compromising on the accuracy.
- Do not lock tables and indexes over extended period of time.
- Performance scales linearly as resources are added.

Configuring the Checkstorage

The step-by-step procedure to configure the checkstorage is explained below. We have considered "test" database as a target database for running the dbcc checkstorage command.

Step 1: Planning resources

In order to run dbcc checkstorage, the Adaptive server needs additional workspaces, worker processes. Also the size of the dbccdb database and devices depends on the size of the databases being checked.

In order to plan for the resources use the system procedure sp_plan_dbccdb.

```
>sp_plan_dbccdb (test)
>go
```

```
Recommended size for dbccdb database is 14MB (data = 12MB, log =
2MB).
dbccdb database already exists with size 1000MB.
Recommended values for workspace size, cache size and process
count are:
dbname              scan     ws text   ws cache process count
test                64K      48K       640K     1
```

```
(return status = 0)
```

The information is also suggestive, meaning that the output provides information about available devices on which you can create dbccdb database.

Note that we need:

a scan workspace of size 64K
a text workspace of size 48K
16 K buffer pool of size 640K
We need a minimum of one worker processe.
The minimum size of the dbccdb database is14MB

Step 2: Configuring Worker processes

By default, the Adaptive server is configured for zero workerprocesses. Change the configuration settings as per the recommendation of the sp_plan_dbccdb output.

```
>sp_configure "number of worker processes", 1
>go
```

```
Parameter Name
         Default  Memory Used        Config Value
         Run      Value              Unit
         Type
   ------------------------------------------------------------
   ---------------------- ---------------------- ----------------
--------
   ------------------------  ------------------------------------
----
   --------------------

number of worker processes

                      0        198       1
                      1        number
         dynamic

(1 row affected)
(return status = 0)
```

Step 3: Setting up a named cache (optional)

By default, the server performs extent reads on dbccdb database and the data pages are read into a 16K buffer pool.

You can create a 16K buffer pool on the "Default Data Cache" or you can configure a dedicated named cache which is dedicated to dbccdb. This improves performance.

```
>sp_cacheconfig dbccdb_cache, "2M"
>go
```

Step 4: Configure a 16K Buffer pool

For optimum performance, the Adaptive server performs extent level reads from the target database. So you need a 16K buffer pool for large IO reads.

Configure the 16K buffer pool on dbccdb_cache.

```
>sp_poolconfig "dbccdb_cache", "640K", "16K"
>go
```

Step 5:Installing dbccdb database

As per the recommendations of sp_plan_dbccdb system procedure, create two new devices for the dbccdb database.

To create a device for placing the data segment of the dbccdb database

```
>disk init
>name = 'dbccdb_data_dev',
>physname = '/sybase/data/dbccdb_data_dev.dat',
>size = '20m'
>go
```

To create a device for placing the logsegment of the dbccdb database

```
>disk init
>name = 'dbccdb_log_dev',
>physname = '/sybase/data/dbccdb_log_dev.dat',
>size = '20m'
>go
```

Create the dbccdb database

```
>create database dbccdb
>on dbccdb_data_dev ='16m'
>log on dbccdb_log_dev ='2m'
>go
```

Then execute the script installdbccdb. This script creates a number of dbccdb system tables and stored procedures.

Path:$SYBASE/$SYBASE_ASE/scripts

Run the script from the isql utility

isql -Usa –P*** -S TEST_2K – i installdbccdb

Then bind the database "dbccdb" to the named cache.

```
>sp_bindcache dbccdb_cache, dbccdb
>go
```

Step 6: Adding Workspace Segments (optional)

A workspace is a table allocated for dbcc storage. The dbcc checkstorage needs two workspace tables.

A scan workspace table for the target database which contains a row for each scanned page.

An additional workspace is needed for the target database when it needs to scan a page that contains a text or image data type.

When we configure the workspace, by default the workspace tables are created in the "default" segment. For good performance create two segments and place them on two separate devices.

Create two devices to place the segments:

```
>disk init
>name = scan_dbcc_dev,
>physname = '/sysbase/data/scan_dbcc_dev.dat',
>size = '5M'
```

```
>go

>disk init
>name = text_dbcc_dev,
>physname = '/sysbase/data/text_dbcc_dev.dat',
>size = '5M'
>go
```

Then add the segments,

```
>sp_addsegment scan_seg, dbccdb, scan_dbcc_dev
>go

>sp_addsegment test_seg, dbccdb, text_dbcc_dev
>go
```

Step 7: Creating the workspaces (optional)

When we run the scrip installdbccdb, by default scan and test workspaces are created. The name of the scan workspace is **def$scan$ws** and its size is 256K.

The name of the test workspace is **def$test$ws** and its size is 128K.

If we do not explicitly configureworkspace tables, these tables will be used. However, if more than two checkstorage operations are performed, each large database requires its own workspace.

As per the recommendations we have derived from the procedure sp_plan_dbcc, let us create workspaces,

```
>sp_dbcc_createws    dbccdb,    scan_seg,    scan_test,    scan,
"80K"
>go

>sp_dbcc_createws    dbccdb,    test_seg,    text_test,    test,
"48K"
>go
```

Where scan_test and text_test are the workspace tables with size 80K and 48K respectively.

The checkstorage operation makes entry for each page scanned, in the workspace tables. The checkstorage operation may fail if the workspace tables are filled.

In order to make room for the automatic expansion of the workspace tables, we need to update the configuration tables in the dbccdb database.

Use sp_dbcc_updateconfig procedure to allow for the automatic expansion of workspace.

```
>sp_dbcc_updateconfig test,"enable automatic workspace expansion", '1'
>go
```

Step 8: Update the attributes of target database

Once dbccdb database workspace tables are created, you need to update the dbcc_config table. You need to update each dbcc parameter separately for each target database.

```
>use dbccdb
>go
>sp_dbcc_updateconfig test, "max worker processes", "1"
>go

>sp_dbcc_updateconfig test,"dbcc named cache", dbccdb_cache, "2K"
>go

>sp_dbcc_updateconfig test, "scan workspace", scan_test
>go

>sp_dbcc_updateconfig test, "text workspace", text_test
>go
```

Step 9: Re-evaluating the setup

It may be required to re-evaluate the configuration information for the target database and compare with the present configuration information. This maybe necessary if the characteristics of the user database changes. Use the procedure sp_dbcc_evaluatedb to evaluate the configuration information.

```
>sp_dbcc_evaluatedb test
```

```
>go
```

```
Recommended values for workspace size, cache size and process
count are:

Database name : test

                              Current               suggested
scan workspace size :         0K                    64K
text workspace size :         0K                    48K
cache size :                  2K                    640K
process count :               2                     1

(return status = 0)
```

Finally perform the checkstorage operation

```
>dbcc checkstorage (test)
>go
```

```
Checking test: Logical pagesize is 2048 bytes
Too many worker processes (2) are configured for the available
16K buffer pool.
This buffer pool can only support 1 workers.
Storage checks for 'test' are complete. DBCC is now recording the
results in the
dbccdb database.
DBCC CHECKSTORAGE for database 'test' sequence 1 completed at Feb
20 2014
7:14PM. 0 faults and 0 suspect conditions were located. 0 checks
were aborted .
You should investigate the recorded faults, and plan a course of
action that
will correct them.
```

Generating Reports from dbccdb

sp_dbcc_summaryreport: Provides summary report for all dbcc checkstorage operations completed for a target database.

```
>sp_dbcc_summaryreport
>go
```

```
DBCC Operation : checkstorage
=================================================================
============= ===
Database Name
         Start time                    End Time
         Operation ID Hard Faults Soft Faults Text Columns Abort
         Count User Name
   ------------------------------------------------------------
   ----------------------------------------  --------------------
------
   ------------ ----------- ----------- ------------ -----------
   ------------------------------------------------------------
test
         02/20/2014 19:14:43                    19:14:48:100
                  1        0        0        0        0
         sa
(1 row affected)
=================================================================
============= ===
(return status = 0)
```

sp_dbcc_fullreport: This procedure inturn runs several other procedures to get a complete picture of the dbcc operations that happened.

```
>sp_dbcc_fullreport
>go
```

image

sp_dbcc_faultreport: This generates the faults occured on a target's database objects that occured.

```
>sp_dbcc_faultreport short, test
>go
```

image

Verify the faults using dbcc checkverfy command.

Example:

```
>dbcc checkverify (test)
>go
```

```
Verifying faults for 'test'.
DBCC CHECKVERIFY for database 'test' sequence 1 completed at Feb
20 2014
7:23PM. 0 suspect conditions considered, 0 identified as faults,
0 identified asharmless, and 0 could not be checked. 0 objects
could not be checked.
```

This operates on the results of the last completed checkstorage operation for the target database.

Cleaning dbccdb

The adaptive server appends data generated by dbcc checkstorage in dbccdb database. As a maintenance task regularly clean up the dbccdb database by using the procedure sp_dbcc_deletehistory

When the target database is deleted, all the configuration information and the checkstorage results related to the target database must be deleted. Use the system procedure sp_dbcc_deletedb to delete all the information form dbccdb related to the target database.

Dropping a Damaged Database

If the database has a large number of inconsistencies or there are any device failures, the adaptive server automatically considers the database as corrupted and it is marked as suspect. In this case you cannot drop the damaged database in a normal way.

Use the dbcc dbrepair command to drop the suspect database.

Example:

```
>dbcc dbrepair (database_name, dropdb)
>go
```

CHAPTER –11

NAMED CACHE

We know that the data cache is a portion of the Adaptive server's shared memory which is used for loading data pages, index pages and log pages from the disk. For an application to read or modify a piece of data , basically the data should be read into the data cache and then the server processes the data. Once the data is processed the data pages are not immediately written back to the disk. The adaptive server manages the memory very efficiently. In the sense by applying LRU algorithm the server efficiently retains busy data in memory and flushes out the not so busy data. By retaining busy data in memory, the server avoids frequent read/write from the disk. This reduces the physical I/O contributing to the improvement in the server's performance.

Performance issues with Data cache

Even though the LRU strategy is designed to keep the busy pages in the data cache memory, in a multiuser environment, running reports and tempdb activity can displace the most popular data out of the data cache. This triggers fresh data read from the disk and this could be problematic.

This is indicated by the high turn over in the sp_sysmon report.

Hash Table

The data cache is associated with a buffer hash table. The buffer hash table contains a list of buffers, through which the adaptive server determines whether a buffer is currently busy or free to read a new page into the cache. If a page is not found in the hash table, then it means that the page is not in the cache and the server needs to make a physical I/O request to read the page into the cache from the disk.

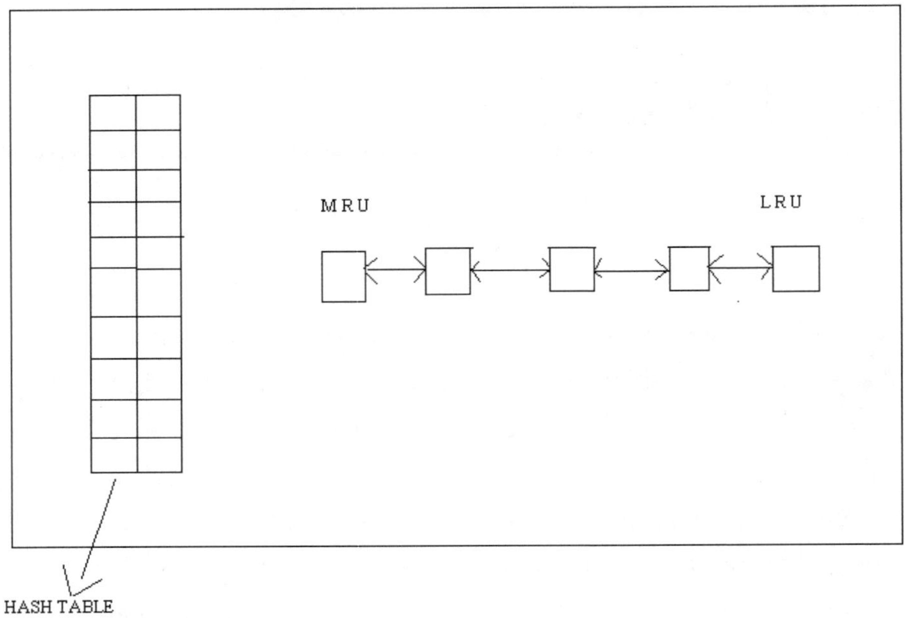

In simpler words, when the user requests for data, the adaptive server needs to first access the hash table even before accessing the data page from the data cache.

When the adaptive server is configured for multiple engines, the server applies spin locks to the buffer hash table to avoid simultaneous access by other engines. This is a wait event, where spin lock contention occurs which makes the engines to wait to access the hash table.

The solution to reduce high turnover due to popular page displacement and to reduce spin lock contention is to configure **named caches**.

What to watch out for?

You need to analyze and judge whether we need to configure a numed cache.

Run the sp_sysmon and filter the report to obtain information about data cache management.

Example:

```
>sp_sysmon "00:00:30", dcache

===============================================================
===============
   Sybase Adaptive Server Enterprise System Performance Report
===============================================================
===============

Server Version:           Adaptive  Server  Enterprise/15.7.0/EBF
                          19495     SMP     /P/x86_64/Enterprise
                          Linux/ase157/2820/64-bit/FBO/Fri   Sep
                          16 00: 54:35 2011
Run Date:                  Mar 26, 2014
Sampling Started at:       Mar 26, 2014 14:39:44
Sampling Ended at:         Mar 26, 2014 14:40:14
Sample Interval:           00:00:30
Sample Mode:               No Clear
Counters Last Cleared:     Mar 24, 2014 10:23:49
Server Name: Test
===============================================================
===============
===============================================================
===============

Data Cache Management
---------------------

Cache Statistics Summary (All Caches)
-------------------------------------
                                    per sec   per xact   count %
of total
                                   ---------  ---------  ------
----------
Cache Search Summary
         Total Cache Hits           25956.9  194676.5 778706
96.6 %
```

```
        Total Cache Misses          906.4    6798.3   27193


3.4 %
------------------------- ------------ ------------ ----------
Total Cache Searches                26863.3  201474.8 805899

Cache Turnover
        Buffers Grabbed             19485.3  146140.0 584560
n/a
        Buffers Grabbed Dirty       0.0      0.0      0
0.0 %

Cache Strategy Summary
        Cached (LRU) Buffers        20188.3  151412.5 605650
44.6 %
        Discarded (MRU) Buffers     25073.2  88049.3  752197
55.4 %

Large I/O Usage
                                    0.0      0.0      0
n/a

Large I/O Effectiveness
        Pages by Lrg I/O Cached     0.0      0.0      0
n/a

Asynchronous Prefetch Activity
        APFs Issued                 18481.1  138608.5 554434
75.5 %
APFs Denied Due To
        APF I/O Overloads           0.1      0.8      3
0.0 %
        APF Limit Overloads         9.9      74.3     297
0.0 %
        APF Reused Overloads        0.2      1.5      6
0.0 %
APF Buffers Found in Cache
        With Spinlock Held          86.8     651.0    2604
0.4 %
        W/o Spinlock Held           5886.5   44148.5  176594
24.1 %
```

```
-------------------------------- ------- ------- ------
Total APFs Requested             24464.6 183484.5 733938
```

Look out for cache hits and misses. Consistently low value of cache hits means that enough memory is not allocated for the data cache.

- Significantly higher cache turnover means data pages are frequently aged out.
- A higher value of spinlock contention (in a multiple engine environment). The solution for this is to create a named cache and cache partition.

NAMED CACHE AND THEIR BENEFITS

A named cache is a user defined cache with its own buffer pool. A named cache is similar to "Default Data Cache", in the sense that it contains a hash table and MRU/LRU chain of data page buffers.

Note that by creating a named cache, we are not partitioning the data cache and carving out a space for named cache.

The default data cache is independent and it exists always and you cannot drop the "Default Data Cache". By default all the objects are implicitly bound to the "Default Data Cache".

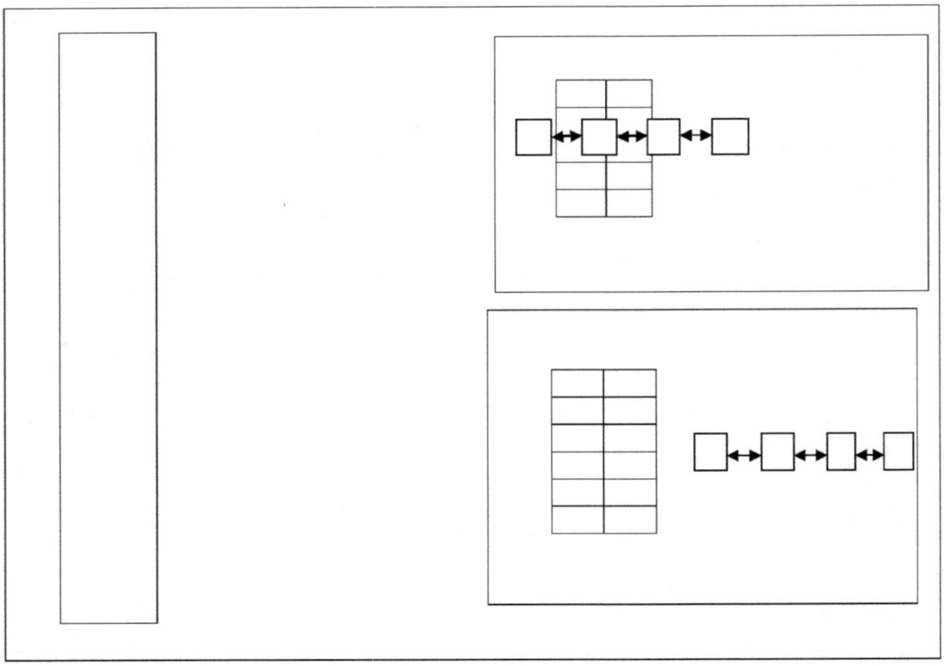

Use system stored procedure sp_helpcache to obtain information about the existing cache and object binding status.

```
>Sp_helpcache
>go
```

To create a named cache, issue:

```
>sp_cacheconfig test_cache, '10M'
>go
```

```
The change is completed. The option is dynamic and ASE need not
be rebooted for
the change to take effect.
(return status = 0)
```

The test_cache is created dynamically and it does not need server reboot. Issue sp_helpcache to confirm the creation of named cache.

<u>Benefits</u>

- Creating exclusive named cache gives you the ability to place critical tables or indexes in memory. Caches with large I/O buffers can significantly quicken table scan and improve large query performance.
- You can bind a hot table to one cache and the indexes of the table to other caches to increase the concurrency.
- If there is a very heavy usage of tempdb, you can bind the tempdb to its own named cache, thereby isolating tempdb to form other user processes.
- You can exclusively bind the database's log segment (syslogs table) to its own cache, thereby reducing the contention.

Binding and Unbinding Objects

In order to bind an object to the named cache, use sp_bindcache.

Example:

```
>sp_bindcache test_cache, test
>go
```

```
(return status = 0)
```

```
>sp_helpcache test_cache
>go
```

```
Cache Name                Config Size                Run Size
        Overhead
------------------------ -------------------------- -----------
--------

                  --------------------

test_cache                10.00 Mb           10.00 Mb
        1.29 Mb

(1 row affected)

------------------ Cache Binding Information: ------------------

Cache Name        Entity Name        Type      Index Name
        Status
                  ----------        --------   -------------

------
test_cache test database
```

```
(return status = 0)
```

You could see that the database test itself is bound to the test_cache.

To unbind a cache, use sp_unbindcache_all

Example:

```
>sp_unbindcache_all test_cache
>go
```

Restrictions

- You must be in the master database to bind or unbind a database.
- An object can be bound to only one cache.
- If the syslogs table is bound to a named cache, then the attributes of the named cache must be log only cache.

To change the size of the named cache, use sp_cacheconfig.

Example:

```
>sp_cacheconfig test_cache, '20M'
>go
```

The following example converts the cache type from mixed cache to logonlycache.

```
>sp_cacheconfig test_cache, 'logonly'
>go
```

To drop a named cache, use sp_cacheconfig.

Example:

```
>sp_cacheconfig test_cache, "0"
>go
```

Use sp_helpcache to confirm that there are no objects bound to test_cache. Unbind the objects before dropping the named cache.

Restrictions:

- The default data cache must always exist and it cannot be dropped.

- The memory of a dropped cached can only be reused after server restart.

SPIN LOCKS AND CACHE PARTITIONING

When the Adaptive server is configured for multiple engines, several tasks will be running in parallel across several engines. However, no matter any number of tasks are running on multiple engines, the cache can only accept one process at a time. The access to the cache is controlled by a special lock structure called spin lock.

A task that needs access to the cache places a lock on the hash table of the cache and accesses the data within the cache. If another task on another engine wants to access the same cache it needs to wait until the lock is released on the hash table. The queued process will enter into spin. The purpose of spin lock is to prevent interference between two running tasks.

Note that the spin lock contention happens only in a multiple engine environment

Reducing Spin Lock Contention

Creating named caches may reduce the spin lock contention. But it is not guaranteed. If there are more hot tables and indexes on a single default cache then you can create multiple named caches and distribute the hot tables and indexes across the named caches. In this case the spin lock contention reduces.

However if there is only one hot table and all the processes running across multiple engines want to access the same hot table, if you create a named cache it will not reduce the spin lock contention. This is because a single table can only bound to a single cache. So if you move the hot table from "Default Data Cache" to another named cache, you are merely shifting the spin lock contention form one cache to another.

In this case the solution is to go for cache partitioning.

Cache Partitioning

The cache partitioning allows a cache to be partitioned into sub-caches or "Cachelets". Each cachelet will have its own hash table.

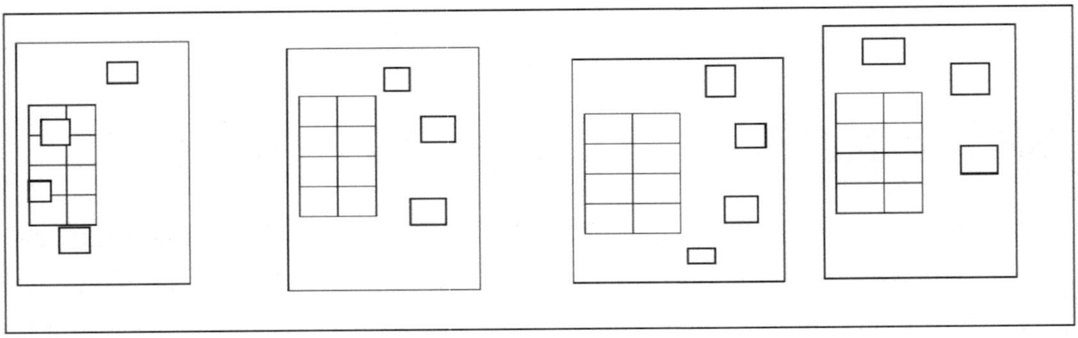

Use sp_cacheconfig system procedure to create cache partitions.

Example

```
>sp_cacheconfig test_cache, "cache_partition" = 4
>go
```

Once the server is rebooted, test_cache will be subdivided into four sections. Or by using the configuration parameter "Global Cache Partition Number", you can configure the server to partition the cache.

Example:

```
>sp_configure "global cache partition number", 4
>go
```

As it is a static parameter, the server must be restarted for the partition to be affected. Now only named cache including the "Default Data Cache" will be automatically partitioned, to four cachelets are created.

Large I/O Buffer Pool

The "Default Data Cache" and every named cache will have a buffer pool. When we read the page from the disk, actually the data is read into a buffer. For example, for a 2K page server, the logical page is 2048(2KBytes) and it is initialized at the device level. In order to read a 2K page into the data cache, 2K buffer must be available in the cache. So every cache will have a default cache pool of 2K buffer and this cannot be altered.

The minimum size of the buffer pool is 256 pages or 512KB for a 2K page server, i.e, a buffer pool can have at least 256 buffers.

Within a cache we can create a separate buffer pool for a large I/O in addition to the default buffer pool. For example we can create a buffer pool of buffer size 4K, 8K or 16K.

The additional buffer pool can be created for a cache using the system procedure sp_poolconfig.

Example:

```
>sp_poolconfig test_cache, "8M", "4K"
>go
```

This command creates a buffer pool of size 8M with I/O size 4K. This means when you access data from the disk, you can read 2 pages in a single disk I/O call and load the pages into the buffer.

This is depicted in the figure below

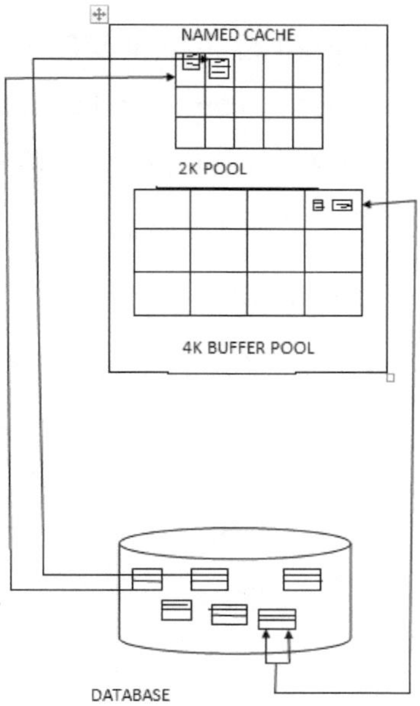

Need for Large I/O buffer Pool

It is possible to improve the query performance by configuring multiple buffer pools to perform large I/O. Whenever the application reads sequential data, they derive a huge performance benefit by reading more number of pages simultaneously in a single disk I/O call. This greatly reduces the number of disk I/O access calls made by the server.

Large /O will enhance the performance in the case of:

- bcp operations
- running dbcc as part of regular maintenance task
- join conditions between large table
- queries that perform range based scans
- batches that read and modify a large number of pages

Note that when multiple buffer pools are configured within a cache, the total size of the buffer pools cannot exceed the size of the cache.

When a large I/O buffer pool is created within a cache, the required memory is taken from the 2K buffer pool and allocated to the large I/O buffer pool.

For example if the data cache size is 100MB, entire 100MB is allocated to the 2k default buffer pool. If you create additional I/O buffer pool of size 30MB, then the 2K buffer pool size is reduced to 70MB and 30MB of memory is allocated to the large I/O buffer pool. This space re-organization between the buffer pools within the cache is dynamic and it does not require server reboot.

Use sp_poolconfig system procedure to modify the buffer pool.

Example:

```
>sp_poolconfig test_cache , "10M", "4K"
```

This command increases the size of the 4K buffer pool to 10MB.

To drop a buffer pool, issue:

```
>sp_poolconfig test_cache, "0", "4K"
>go
```

After dropping a buffer pool, the memory is readjusted with the default buffer pool.

Final Word About Named caches

Cache reconfiguration should only be performed when you have a specific performance problem. Before turning and configuring the cache, consistently analyze the sp_sysmon reports.

Note that reducing spin lock contention may not be achieved by using named caches.

Random data access in a OLTP environment are not benefited by configuring large I/O buffer pools.

CHAPTER – 12

ENHANCEMENTS IN SYBASE ASE - VERSION 15.5 AND 15.7

KERNEL MODE

As of ASE version 15.7, Sybase has introduced two kernels. Namely:

Threaded Kernel

Process Kernel

The default kernel mode is threaded kernel. You could view the information with a global variable **@@kernelmode.**

Example:

```
>select @@Kernelmode
>go
```

As we know that each engine configured for the Adaptive server is an independent operating system process. The engines are operating system processes which cooperate with each other to share Adaptive server's workload.

Process Mode

The process kernel mode is used in versions prior to Sybase ASE 15.7 and it is retained as a risk mitigation plan. As we know, each process in the process mode kernel is an engine.

In a multiple processor environment, ASE runs as a multiple operating system process that will cooperate and interact with each other to work as a single server. Meaning that any task can migrate between engines and engines themselves can migrate between CPUs.

However,

- The network I/Os are distributed across engines and engines are bound to a network I/O. That means a network I/O for a connection should be performed by an engine which has a connection.
- If an engine issues a disk I/O access call, then the task must be completed by that engine.

The network I/O and disk I/O calls cannot migrate between engines. These operations are improved in Sybase ASE 15.7 by introducing threaded kernel mode.

Threaded Kernel Mode

- Better streamlined I/O handling, thereby reducing wait events leading to no wastage of CPU cycles. Hence the threaded kernel mode uses significantly less CPU than the process mode.
- The new threaded kernel delivers a consistent performance in mixed work load and task to engine affinity is greatly reduced.

The notable difference is that when you choose the Adaptive server to start in a threaded mode, it appears as a single process in your Operating system (however in process mode, it appears as multiple processes on the operating system).

In the context of threaded kernel mode, we redefine the engine on a thread (not as a process) in a thread pool. All the threads exist in a thread pool by name syb_default_pool.

Actually all the user and system tasks run in the syb_default_pool.

Changing the Kernel Mode

The default kernel mode is threaded kernel mode.

Example:

```
>select @@kernelmode
>go
```

The kernel mode can be changed by changing the configuration parameter "Kernel Mode".

Example:

```
>sp_configure 'kernel mode', 0, process
>go
```

It is a static parameter and ASE must be restarted.

Note that we have the option of switching back to process kernel mode as a risk mitigation. You can adapt to threaded kernel mode without any changes to applications.

IN-MEMORY DATABASE

The traditional databases are disk resident databases, which employ disk storage mechanism. In applications involving reporting mechanisms where the response time is very critical and data durability is not a question, you can use in-memory database.

An in-memory database is a database management system that is completely resident on the shared memory. The in-memory databases were introduced since Sybase ASE version 15.5.

The following example gives a procedure to create an in memory database

Step 1: Create In-memory cache

Before creating the in-memory database, we need to create in-memory cache. This is accomplished by using the system procedure sp_cacheconfig.

```
>sp_cacheconfig
test_imdb_cache,'40M',inmemory_storage,'none','cache_par
tition = 2'
```

```
>go
```

Step 2: Create a virtual disk in the cache.

A virtual disk needs to be created in the cache memory so as to create the In-memory database

```
>disk init
>name='test_imdb_dev',
>physname = 'test_imdb_cache',
>size = '20M'
>type = 'inmemory'
>go
```

This creates a virtual disk on the memory storage cache test_imdb_cache.

Step 3: Create an in-memory database

```
>Create inmemory database test_imdb
on test_imdb_dev = '10M'
with durability = no_recovery
>go
```

As of Sybase ASE 15.7, the server supports the following durability levels:

full – This is the default option for disk resident databases. This means all the committed transactions are written to the disk, and ensures full recovery during server failures.

no_recovery– the transactions are durable only when the server is up and running. The transactions are lost if the server fails or even when the clean shutdown of the server is performed.

The in-memory databases are supported only with the durability option no_recovery. This means that the in-memory databases are not recoverable. So in-memory databases are not a choice for OLTP applications!

However the in-memory databases can be recreated by using the model database as a template when the server is restarted.

at_shutdown – The transactions are durable when the server is up and running and the transactions are durable even after a clean shutdown of the Adaptive server.

But the transactions are lost if the server fails and it is not recoverable.

As of ASE version 15.7, creating in-memory databases with durability **at_shutdown** is not supported.

Creating Databases with Data Compression

ASE version 15.7 introduces data compression. This lets you to use less storage space for the same amount of data, thereby reducing cache memory consumption and improve performance.

The salient features of data compression are:

- Data compression is supported for APL and DOL tables.
- Data compression option can be chosen at the row level or page level.
- Compression allowed for LOB data.
- Compression can be defined at database level or at table level.

Compression Option with Create Database Command

Syntax:

```
>create database <database_name>
on <device_name> = 'size'
with compression = page/row/none
with lob_compression = compression_level
```

none – Data is not compressed

row – The Adaptive server stores data in a row compressed form

page – Adaptive server compresses data at the page level only after it has compressed data at the row level. So if we choose compression at the page level, it will also compress data at the row level.

Example:

```
>create database test_db
on test_dev = '50M'
with compression = page
```

```
>create database test_lob_db
on test_lob_dev = '50M'
with lob_compression = 101
```

Shrinking the Transaction log

Sybase has met a long standing requirement of shrinking the transaction log!

You may need to accommodate for the expansion of the transaction log to come out of log fill situations. As Sybase now allows fully recoverable DMLs for a few operations, you may need to allow one time operations which need a lot of log space.

Now, as of ASE version 15.7, you can shrink the transaction log, thereby removing the unwanted log space.

The following example illustrates shrinking log space.

Create a database by name test on multiple log devices.

```
>create database test
on test_dev = 5
log on test_log1_dev = 3, test_log2_dev = 3,
test_log3_dev = 3
>go
```

```
View the size of the database using the system procedure
```

```
>sp_helpdb test
>go
```

The total size of the database is 14MB with data segment being 5MB and the transaction log segment is fragmented across three devices.

```
>select * from sysusages
where segmap = 4
and
dbid = db_id ('test')
```

```
>go
```

The query shows that the log segment is spread across three devices.

Now shrink the log using alter database command.

```
>alter database test log off tes_log3_dev
>go
```

Rerun the query on sysusage system table. You could see that the segment on the device test_log3_dev is completely removed.

NEW DATABASE OPTIONS

Full logging for all – Prior to ASE version 15.7, creating a copy table using select into, adding a non null column using alter table and reorg rebuild were done in a minimally logged mode. Before running these operations, we were made to change the database property to minimally logged mode by setting the database option "**select into/blk copy/pll sort**", to **"true".**

But this has a disadvantage as it would invalidate the transaction log sequence. You were forced to reinitiate the backup by performing full database dump. This is undesirable for large databases.

Now with ASE version 15.7, you can opt for full logging database option and run a few operations in a full logged mode. This does not break the transaction log dump sequence.

Example:

```
>sp_dboption <database_name> "full logging for select into", 'true'
>go
```

Creating proxy tables in a remote server, data movement between two tables in a local server can be now performed in fully logged mode.

```
>sp_dboption <database_name>, 'full logging for alter table', 'true'
```

```
>go
```

This allows full logged operations for adding or dropping column with not null property.

```
>sp_dboption <database_name>, 'full logging for reorg rebuild', 'true'
>go
```

As you know, reorg rebuild operation on a table involves table's data movement. This option enables table data movement in a full logged mode.

```
>sp_dboption <database_name>, 'full logging for all', 'true'
>go
```

This option enables full logging for all the above operations. If this dboption is set to 'true', there is no need to individually set full logging for select into, alter table, reorg build.

Restrictions: Note that full logging operation is still not supported for fast bcp operations and parallel sort operations. To perform fast bcp and parallel sort we still need to set the dboption "select into/bulk copy/pll sort" to true.

You cannot set full logging for master database and in-memory databases.

Enforce dump tran Sequence

```
>sp_dboption <database_name>, 'enforce dump tran sequence', 'true'
>go
```

When this option is set to"**true",** the database does not allow any operations that needs minimally logged mode.

Thus, the database options 'select into/bulk copy/pll sort' and 'enforce dump tran sequence' are mutually exclusive and both cannot be true.

Other effects are:

The transaction log cannot be truncated by the checkpoint process when 'trunc log on chkpt' is enabled.

The execution of 'dump tran with truncate_only' and 'dump tran with no_log' does not truncate the transaction log. The log can only be truncated by dumping the transaction log to an archive device.

You cannot make the database as read_only.

CHAPTER – 13

CLIENT UTILITIES

Sybase ASE is a client-server architecture where a client program connects to the Adaptive server and sends commands, The adaptive server accesses and manipulates the data and the processed data is returned to the client. In order to communicate with the Adaptive server, ASE comes with its own utilities. The utility programs are commands that are invoked directly from the operating system.

In this chapter, we introduce important utility programs.

DDLGEN

The ddlgen utility is a Java-based tool used for generating definitions for server and database level objects in Adaptive server.

The installation program ships the ddlgen executables and it is available in the path $SYBASE/ASEP/bin.

To view the current version of the ddlgen invoke ddlgen from the operating system prompt and issue:

$ ./ddlgen -v

```
Sybase Adaptive Server Enterprise DDL Generator Utility/15.7/EBF
19497/S/1.6.0/ase157/Fri Sep 16 02:05:32 PDT 2011
```

To connect to the server you need to pass the parameters:

-U<login>
-P<password>
-S <host_name:port_number>

You need to specify the host number or IP address along with the port number. Note that -S option is mandatory, because ddlgen does not connect to a default server.

The following examples demonstrate the usage of ddlgen utility. We assume that the host name is localhost and portnumber is 5000, and user is “sa”.

Example 1

Invoke ddlgen and issue:

```
$ ./ddlgen -Usa -P -Slocalhost:5000
```

As the database name is not specified , the ddlgen utility by default connects to the master database and generates DDL for the master database. The DDLs are not captured in the output file and it is displayed at the console.

Example 2

The following command generates DDLs for pubs2 database and the DDLs are captured in a file.

```
$ ./ddlgen -Usa -P –Slocalhost:5000 -Dpubs2 -o$SYBASE/ddl/pubs2_ddl.txt
```

Here the option -D specifies the default database.

Alternatively, you can issue:

```
$ ./ddlgen -Usa -P -Slocalhost:5000 -TDB -Npubs2 -
o$SYBASE/ddl/pubs2_ddl.txt
```

Here,

DB stands for Database
N stands for name of the object
T stands for the type of the object

The type of object can be:

U -table
I -index
V -view
R -rule
P -stored procedures
TR -trigger
USR -user

Combine any of the objects with the type T and exclusively specify the name of the object with the parameter -N.

Example 3

To generate the DDL for the table titles in the pubs2 database, use

```
$ ./ddlgen -Usa -P -Slocalhost:5000 -Dpubs2 -TU -Ntitles
```

Apart from generating DDLs for the table titles, the ddlgen also produces the DDLs for the associated indexes, triggers and all the associated object level permissions are generated.

Example 4

To generate the DDL for the indexes of the table titles issue:

```
$ ./ddlgen -Usa -P -Slocalhost:500 -TI -Dpubs2 -Ntitles.%
```

BCP

The Bulk Copy Program or bcp is a high speed utility used for transferring data between a database table or a view and an operating system file.

The uses of bcp are:

- transferring data from one server to other server in a data migration operations
- load balancing into partitioned tables

- copying data out of a view
- to import data associated with other RDMs
- maintaining tables level backups without using dump and load commands

The Adaptive server can accept data in any character format or binary format.

Requirements for bcp

Before starting the BCP operation, you need to provide the information related to data transfer and need to pass necessary commands to access data.

You must specify

- name of the database
- name of the table or view
- name of the operating system file
- the direction of the data transfer
- to export data from a table you should have select permission on the table, select permission on system tables syssubjects, syscolumns and sysindexes.

Bcp modes

The bcp operations can basically work in two modes namely.

Fast bcp
Slow bcp

You cannot explicitly specify the bcp speed as fast bcp or slow bcp. The server performs either fast bcp or slow bcp based on the indexes and triggers associated with the table.

Fast bcp: When fast bcp is performed, the Adaptive server does not generate transaction log records for bulk inserts. So fast bcp will fail on databases which do not allow for minimally logged operations.

To allow fast bcp, set the database option "selectinto/bulkcopy/pllsort" to true.

Example:

```
>sp_dboption <database_name>, 'selectinto/bulkcopy/pllsort',
'true'
>go
```

The fast bcp only logs page allocation information in the transaction log.

If there are indexes and triggers associated with the target table, the server automatically chooses slow bcp.

So in addition to changing the database option to minimally logged mode, in order to force fast bcp you must either remove or disable triggers from the target table. Also remove indexes from the target table.

Since bulk inserts are not logged, the fast bcp provides a better performance. For extremely large tables forcing fast bcp is a preferred choice.

Restrictions: Since the bulk inserts are not logged, the transaction log dump cannot be performed on the target database. This would break the transaction log dump sequence. So you must dump the entire database.

Slow bcp: All the inserts are logged into the transaction log. However, data insertion is very slow and performance suffers. It is not a realistic choice to perform bcp operations on large tables. Keeping indexes and triggers on the target table causes the server to choose slow bcp.

Note that the distinction between the fast bcp and slow bcp will apply while loading data into a table. This does not apply when performing bcp out(copying data from a table)

bcp file format

You can copy the contents of a table using bcp in two different formats.

Character format : The data from the table is extracted in the character format and uses the character database for all data.

The character format is specified by using -c flag in the bcp command. You can provide tabs between the fields of a row.

The character format is useful when you copy the data and port the data across heterogeneous platforms and different versions of ASE. However the bcp operation will be slow.

Native format: The bcp uses the operating system native format to extract data. The native format can only be used when moving data between the servers with the same operating system. Extracting data in the native format is relatively faster than the character format.

However, note that when extracting the contents of system tables, you should use the only character format.

The following examples illustrate different types of bcp operations.

Example 1: To copy the data from titles table into a operating system file, issue:

```
$ bcp pubs2..titles out $SYBASE/bcp/pubs2_titles.txt -Usa -
Stest -c
password:
```

Example 2: Copies data out of authors table in the pubs2 database in the character format. Each field is ended with a :(colon) and each row is ended with a Return.

```
$bcp pubs2..authors out $SYBASE/bcp/authors.txt -Usa -
S<server_name>
-c -t -r \\r
```

Example 3: The data is loaded into the table titles from data file pubs2_titles.txt.

```
$bcp pubs2..titles in $SYBASE/bcp/pubs2_titles.txt -Usa
-S<server_name> -c -J
```

The option -J specifies the client character set. The bcp uses a filter to convert the data input between the client character set and the character set used by the adaptive server.

Bcp Recovery

If the server fails when a bcp operation is being performed, the server rolls back the bcp and no data is inserted into the table, and you need to redo the work.

For large tables, use the -b option. This will set the batch size so that each batch is treated as an atomic transaction with a checkpoint. In this case, if the server fails, the data is loaded into the table up to the last successfully completed batch.

Example:

```
$bcp test..accounts in accounts_data.txt -Usa -P <password> -
S<server_name> -c -b20000
```

The batch size is 20,000 records.

OPTDIAG

The optdiag is a utility which is used to display optimizer statistics and you can load the updated statistics into system tables as well.

The optdiag displays the information associated with the sysstatistics and systabstats system tables. You could derive the information such as table size, structure of the table, structure of the associated index and the distribution of the data within the columns.

Optdiag Usage

- You can determine and assess the extent of table fragmentation.
- View the column histogram values.
- Get the information about cluster ratios

Complete description and analysis of the optdiag output is beyond the scope of this book. We have given a few examples for generating optimizer statistics using optdiag utility.

Example 1: To display statistics for all user tables of the pubs2 database, issue:

```
$optdiag statistics pubs2 -Usa -P<password> -S<server_name>
-o pubs2_statistics
```

The output is captured in a file.

Example 2: Displays the statistics for titles table of pubs2 database.

```
$optdiag statistics pubs2..titles -Usa -P<password> -S<server_name>
```

Example 3: Displays the statistics for the column name 'title' of table titles.

```
$optdiag statistics pubs2..titles.title -Usa -P<password>
-S<server_name>
```

Example 4: The following option loads the statistics from a file 'titles_statistics' into the system tables.

```
$optdiag statistics -ititles_statistics -Usa -P<password
-S<server_name>
```

The -i option specifies the input mode. You need to specify the input file. The optdiag reads from the file and updates statistics in sysstatistics system table.

CONCLUSION

Reflecting on the journey from basic concepts to the new features in ASE 16.0, I hope you've found practical insights that will enhance your ability to manage and optimize ASE systems. The tips shared here are designed to help you address everyday challenges and maximize the benefits of your Sybase ASE setup.

Now, as you apply these techniques in your work, envision the improvements and efficiencies you'll achieve. This book is meant to be a steppingstone; to continue growing, I encourage you to connect with the Sybase ASE community, engage in forums, and stay informed about the latest developments.

Your expertise with Sybase ASE is a significant asset. By actively using the knowledge gained from this book, you'll strengthen your skills and contribute to the continued success of your organization

Made in the USA
Columbia, SC
09 January 2025

51457060R00135